Keanu Reeves

AN EXCELLENT ADVENTURE

Keanu Reeves

AN EXCELLENT ADVENTURE

Brian J. Robb

PLEXUS, LONDON

Published by Plexus Publishing Limited
55a Clapham Common Southside
London SW4 9BX
First Printing 1997

British Library Cataloguing in Publication Data

Robb, Brian J.
  Keanu Reeves : an excellent adventure
  1. Reeves, Keanu 2. Motion picture actors and
actresses -
  United States - Biography
  I. Title
  791.4'3'028'092

  ISBN 0 85965 245 9

Printed in Great Britain by
Hillman Printers, Frome.
Book design by Mitchell Associates
Cover design by Design Revolution

Acknowledgements

To my brother, Steven.

Thanks to BFI Information and Library Services
and Mike Wingate at C&A Video in Edinburgh.
Other organisations and individuals who
provided additional assistance include: The
Directors Guild of America; American Film
Institute; British Film Institute; National Film
Theatre; all at Plexus and everyone at the
various film production, distributors and
publicists offices.
  I would like to thank the following
magazines and newspapers for their coverage
of Keanu Reeves over the years: *Film Review;
The List; Vox; GQ; Sky Magazine; Esquire;
Attitude; Entertainment Weekly; Sight and
Sound; Empire; Premiere* (US, UK and French
editions); *U.S. Magazine; Vanity Fair; Here!;
People Weekly; Daily Mirror; The Sun; News of
the World; Daily Star; Village Voice; Film Threat;
Fangoria; Cinefantastique; Starlog; Interview;
Vogue; American Film; Time Out; What's On In
London; The Face; Rolling Stone; Hello!; Monthly
Film Bulletin; Time; Movieline; Variety; New
Yorker; TV Guide; Film Monthly; Scotland on
Sunday; The Guardian; The Daily Record; The
Mail on Sunday; The Daily Mail; The Sunday
Telegraph; The Scotsman; The Herald; Today;
The Sunday Times; The Independent; The
Evening Standard; The Daily Telegraph;
Edinburgh Evening News; The Sunday Express;
Spectator; Today; The New York Times; The
Observer* and *The Daily Express.*
  Grateful thanks to the following libraries and
film companies for supplying photographs:
Alpha; All Action; All Action/PAT/Arnal/Garcia;
Philip Ramey/All Action; All Action/Stills/ Foto
Blitz; Jean Cummings/All Action; All
Action/Feature Flash; All Action/Stills/I.P.A;
British Film Institute; Corbis/Everett Collection;
Range/Everett Pictures Limited; Ronald Grant;
Columbia TriStar Films (UK); Castle Premier
Releasing; Columbia Pictures Inc; Entertainment
Films; Takashi Seida/Twentieth Century Fox;
Richard Foreman/Twentieth Century Fox;
Murray Close/Twentieth Century Fox; Steve
Granitz/Retna; Armando Gallo/Retna; Martin
Goodacre/Retna; Bill Davila/Retna; Brad
Fierce/La Moine/Katz Pictures Limited; Steven
Klein/Katz Pictures Limited/Outline; Brad
Fierce/La Moine/Katz Pictures Limited; Alberto
Tolot/Katz Pictures Limited; Brad Fierce/La
Moine/Katz Pictures Limited; Scope
Features/Shooting Star; Alan Markfield/Scope
Features/Shooting Star; Stephen Hamels/Scope
Features/Shooting Star; Takashi Seida/TriStar
Pictures, Inc; People in Pictures; MCP/Time
Out. Cover photograph by Deborah
Feingold/Katz Pictures Limited/Outline.
  Film stills courtesy of Twentieth Century Fox;
Metro-Goldwyn-Mayer; United Artists; Disney;
Lorimar Motion Pictures; CBS Entertainment
Productions; Hemdale Film Corporation; New
Lines; Paramount Pictures; Kings Road; Warner
Brothers; American Playhouse; Universal
Pictures; Chestnut Hill/TriStar; Odyssey/Polar
Entertainment Corporation; Largo
Entertainment; New Line Cinema; Columbia
Pictures; Interscope Communications; American
Zoetrope; Osiris Films; Pandora; BBC;
Renaissance Films; Samuel Goldwyn Company;
Fourth Vision; CiBy 2000; Cinevision; Alliance
Communications; TriStar; Zucker Brothers
Production; Fine Line; Jersey Films; Chicago
Pacific Entertainment; Bates Entertainment;
Kushner Locke Co; Tapestry Films; KI;
7 Venture; New Regency; 3 Arts.

Contents

Introduction

KEANU REEVES has become one of the biggest star names in modern Hollywood, thanks in large part to the runaway success of the blockbuster action movie *Speed*. Prior to that, Keanu was perceived as a teen idol pin-up who had made the genre of teen films his own with the likes of the controversial drama *River's Edge* and the goofy time-travel movie *Bill and Ted's Excellent Adventure*. However, there had always been more to Keanu than the airhead image he projected in these early films.

In contrast, as his career progressed, he also tackled several literary-inspired costume dramas: in *Dangerous Liaisons, Bram Stoker's Dracula* and *Much Ado About Nothing*.

Keanu Reeves has endeavoured to carve out a unique niche for himself, never afraid to experiment and stretch his own abilities, in films such as the controversial gay hustler drama *My Own Private Idaho*, with the late River Phoenix, and the magical realist soap-opera drama *Aunt Julia and the Scriptwriter*.

The films of Keanu Reeves have been nothing if not varied, and whether he's seen as a teen idol or a modern leading man, he's always been ambitious about his craft. He takes the process of acting seriously, being the only one of a group of young Hollywood stars – including Johnny Depp, Brad Pitt, River Phoenix and Christian Slater – to tackle Shakespeare. His interest in the Bard has been evident not only on film, but also on stage, when he took the risk of playing the daunting role of *Hamlet* in Winnipeg in January 1995.

Since *Speed*, Keanu has enjoyed action hero status, playing the role with gusto in the Andrew Davis-directed thriller, *Chain Reaction*, and holding his own opposite such experienced talent as Al Pacino in the satanic legal thriller *Devil's Advocate*. At the same time, Keanu was keen to continue to work in low budget and experimental film with novice directors, such as the character drama *Feeling Minnesota*. He even harbours ambitions of putting together a film on the controversial questions surrounding the authorship of Shakespeare's plays.

In his career to date, he's enjoyed the opportunities of working with acclaimed directors such as Gus Van Sant, Bernardo Bertolucci, Stephen Frears and Francis Ford Coppola. He didn't seek them out – these talented directors, who could have had their pick of any leading man, have actively sought out Keanu Reeves.

While critics have sometimes reluctantly admitted that the likes of Brad Pitt and Johnny Depp can turn in performances above and beyond their good looks, Reeves

Playing for laughs: Alex Winter and Keanu Reeves. Keanu was concerned that audiences couldn't see beyond his 'Ted' persona.

Keanu and River Phoenix took risks with their images and audiences in Gus Van Sant's My Own Private Idaho.

has sometimes been the whipping boy of the young Hollywood set. Criticised as wooden and hopeless on occasion, he rises above it all, continuing to produce blockbuster films that secure his status at the top of the Hollywood tree.

Although Keanu loves to act out in public his airhead persona from *Bill and Ted*, he's a much smarter operator than he cares to reveal, carefully building his Hollywood profile, taking advantage of every opportunity before him and building a strong career on the back of what have been described as limited abilities. 'I'm still learning, dude,' he once told one interviewer. It's an education in the art and craft of movie acting that Keanu has bravely carried out in public, getting better in each film and wiser in his choices of material. However, his urge to try something new, to do something different and contrary to his image has earned him the right to fail now and again. His fans have so far stuck with him no matter what he turns his attentions to.

The ongoing contradiction between what some critics regard as his seeming lack of dramatic ability and his world-wide superstar success says as much about modern Hollywood as it does about this young man who has managed to make the system work to his own advantage. Knowing that image can often outweigh talent (or lack of it), Keanu has wisely played to his strengths over the years, culminating in the tailor-made fusion of image and ability in the runaway success *Speed*.

As a new type of action hero, Keanu made a huge impact in Jan De Bont's thriller Speed.

While some critics complained that Keanu 'couldn't act', his fans and general movie-goers alike lapped up his every appearance, propelling Keanu Reeves to a $10-million-per-movie salary. He was enigmatic on screen and off, a loner who seemed to have no private life, someone onto whom his audiences could project their own desires. Keanu's appeal came from whatever particular audiences were looking for, his image being infinitely adaptable to meet the needs of various groups, from screaming teen girls to his strong, loyal gay fan base.

Although flattered by the attention, Keanu himself can't relate to the fuss that surrounds him. Despite his high public profile, Keanu has been almost paranoid in the secrecy which surrounds his private life. Although variously linked in rumours with Pamela Anderson, Sharon Stone, Sofia Coppola in 1993 and a mysterious actress-model named Autumn Mackintosh, as well as, most recently, Amanda De Cadenet, Keanu has never enjoyed a public, high profile romance. The lack of tangible heterosexual activity, like that of other prominent young movie stars, led to speculation about his sexuality. A homoerotic early role in the theatre in *Wolfboy* and his up-front performance as a hustler in Gus Van Sant's *My Own Private Idaho* did nothing to dampen speculation about Keanu's sexual preferences.

This sexual ambiguity has undoubtedly been part of the Keanu Reeves appeal. He moved on from the 1991 description of his character in *Point Break* ('young, dumb and full of cum') to something less macho and less clearly defined. From his

Keanu poised for action in Point Break.

It's only rock and roll: Keanu's other career as a member of grunge rock band Dogstar.

exotic name to his almost feminine good looks, Keanu has a strong female and gay male following which doesn't necessarily rely on his acting ability to draw fans. His redefinition of male movie sexuality has played into his mysterious off-screen private life, and vice versa. The actor recognises these aspects of his image and appeal: 'I've always played the male equivalent of the female ingenue. I've always played innocents.'

On the way to Hollywood fame and fortune the devil-may-care actor has had several brushes with death due to his obsession with motorbikes and speed, and sports a huge chest-to-navel scar from a near-fatal 1987 crash.

These incidents and several more motorcycle accidents have caused friends and associates to voice fears for his future – is he going to follow the 'bad boy' path of Johnny Depp or the fatal route of drug-addicted River

Phoenix? His rock 'n' roll ambitions with his band Dogstar have also caused his advisers to worry about the newest hot-shot Hollywood mega-dollar star throwing away his lucrative movie career to pursue elusive rock 'n' roll stardom.

Held by Los Angeles police in 1993 on a drunk-driving charge, Keanu was horrified to see that his police mug-shot reminded him of his absent, convicted drug-dealer father Samuel. To a large extent, Keanu's life and relationship difficulties have been defined by the absence of the father he hasn't seen since turning thirteen. It's this early trauma that has provided both the drive behind Keanu's career and the fatal hesitancy he has in committing to long-term relationships. His fear that lovers, advisers and even his audiences will abandon him rules his life.

An enigma in public and in private, Keanu Reeves has gone to great lengths to control his public persona. 'I'm a pure Virgo – order, control, perfectionism,' he has admitted. He picks and chooses his roles with greater care than ever before and works hard to control his press. However, as he reaches his mid-30s, the second half of the actor's career looms – and he has to make some serious decisions about his future. So far it's all been a truly excellent adventure, but now the teen idol has grown up and adulthood looms.

'I'd pay to see Keanu Reeves in leather trousers,' said Kenneth Branagh of his Much Ado About Nothing *co-star.*

CHAPTER ONE

Cool Breeze

KEANU CHARLES REEVES was born on 2 September 1964 in Beirut, Lebanon. In the 1960s the area was a Middle Eastern version of the French Riviera, not the war-torn ruin of today. His father was Samuel Nowlin Reeves, the half-Chinese, half-Hawaiian son of a wealthy Hawaiian island family from Oahu. Samuel, a geologist, was working for an oil company in Beirut when he met, fell in love with and quickly married Patricia, an English-born showgirl whom he first saw perform at a local club. She preferred to be known by the nickname Patric and had trained in London as a theatrical designer.

Staying in Beirut, the couple cut something of a Swinging Sixties dash, with Sam at the wheel of his purple Jaguar XKE and Patricia strutting her stuff in cowboy boots, blue jeans and a mink coat. The funds that fuelled their hedonistic lifestyle came from Keanu's paternal step-grandfather Colman Abrahams, who had made his fortune by publishing a children's edition of the *Encyclopaedia Britannica* in Canada.

It wasn't a lifestyle that was to last long, and the romance was over by the time Keanu was two years old, but not before he had been joined by a younger sister named Kim, whom Keanu was to stay close to all his life. It was from his father that the boy had gained the name that was to add to his star presence and mystery when older. Hawaiian for 'cool breeze over the mountains', the name was about the only thing that Keanu Reeves was to be grateful to his largely absent father for.

Samuel was gone before Keanu really got to know him. 'There were fights about Sam's drug-taking,' related Keanu's cousin, Leslie. 'My aunt [Patricia] grew out of the hippie phase, my uncle didn't. He refused – in fact, he couldn't give up the drugs.' Samuel Reeves's drug habit never left him, and in 1994 he was arrested in Hawaii and sentenced to a decade in prison for heroin and cocaine possession.

With Samuel out of their lives, Patricia, Keanu and Kim headed to Australia for a year, before returning to the United States and settling in New York City. Keanu's sister, Kim, recalls their childhood as being one on the road – they moved house five times in a short period. 'I've no idea why,' she remembered, 'it's not like the houses got bigger or anything.' They enjoyed a happy childhood, though, and one of Kim's fondest memories is of her older brother cheerfully dismantling the family's meagre furniture with his junior tool-set.

In 1970, when Keanu was six, Patricia married her second husband, Broadway and Hollywood director, Paul Aaron. The marriage provoked another family upheaval, with a move to Toronto, where the couple felt it would be better to raise the children. It didn't last, and after less than a year Aaron, too, was gone. The six months or so that Paul Aaron was around, however, served to pique the interest of Keanu Reeves in the performing arts.

All children love to perform for their parents, but when one of your parents is responsible for directing the performances of others for a living, it's a whole different matter. For Keanu, Aaron was the first person in his life who was to view seriously his growing interests. Aaron was as close as Keanu came to having a 'real' father figure to guide him. Later Aaron was to play a crucial part in getting the young actor on the road to success in Hollywood.

With support from her in-laws, who lived nearby in Toronto, Patricia turned her hip '60s fashion sense, her interest in clothes and her training in theatrical design in London into a career as a costume designer. She found employment making clothes for, among others, Emmylou Harris, Dolly Parton and David Bowie. This new professional interest meant, like Samuel, Patricia was not around much for her children. His mother's professional endeavours had welcome side benefits for the young – and even then, theatrical – Keanu, however. 'Halloween was exceptional, because I'd always get a cool costume. One year, I was Dracula and wore this really cool cape. Another year I was Batman and my sister was Robin. Once she made me this Cousin Itt costume, like from *The Addams Family*. I wore this giant wig. It rained that Halloween. I got wet. I just looked like a big bowl of pasta.'

While she struggled to develop her new career, Patricia had two children to bring up largely on her own, and both had learning difficulties. Diagnosed dyslexic, reading and writing proved to be a problem for both Keanu and Kim, as well as for their single mother, but it was something the family strived together to overcome. Later, both children became proficient readers, but the early problems may have given Keanu more of a feel for the visual than the literary. Once he could read, though, Keanu became widely and well-read, a fact somewhat at odds with his seemingly less intellectual public persona. He is also left-handed (as seen clearly in some of the films) which proved to be another point of difference from the other kids around him.

As often as the family moved house and Keanu switched schools, so Patricia would change partners. The family seemed in permanent upheaval, a way of life carried on from Patricia's '60s lifestyle. Keanu's sister Kim remembered the atmosphere in the household being reflective of whichever man was in residence at the time. 'How we lived our lives depended on the man of the moment,' she told *People* magazine. 'When Mom was married to Paul, we dressed in white every Friday night and sang Shabbat songs, and we went to Jewish camps in the summer.'

Every so often Patricia would be called away on business and occasionally, some of her star-name clients would drop in to visit. Keanu and Kim became used to late night, loud parties. When Alice Cooper recorded *Welcome to my*

Nightmare at a nearby studio, he stayed at the Reeves's family home, an event vividly recalled by Keanu's childhood chum and hockey team mate Evan Williams: 'I remember, once, Keanu and I trying to take on Alice Cooper. He tied us up like a human knot.'

Keanu recalled the celebrity visitors and his first brush with the grown-up world of drugs. 'There were times when groovy people would come over. I remember [Cooper] brought fake vomit and dog pooh to terrorise the housekeeper. He'd hang out, a regular dude. We got to go out to concerts and stuff. When I was fifteen, a friend of my mom's took me to see Emmylou Harris, and I got to stay up all night. It was the first time I ever saw a person come out of the bathroom with cocaine on their nostril hair – this guy with a moustache had cocaine all over it. . .'

Keanu seems to have taken it all in his stride, and he seems to have found some much-needed stability at Toronto's Jesse Ketchum Public School, which Keanu attended from Kindergarten through to eighth grade in 1978, aged fourteen. 'I don't think he ever got to class on time,' recalled his teacher, Paula Warder. 'When he did arrive, he wasn't quite, well . . . with it. He always left his books at home or forgot his homework. But he'd just smile and go back home to get them. And somehow he did pass his classes.' One teacher, though, recalled that Keanu would stay behind school and play basketball on his own, until later hooking up with his sister, Kim. It showed a lonely streak in the young Keanu, a reluctance to get too close to friends and a strong connection with his sister.

Despite the fringe show-business background at the house in the Yorkville quarter of Toronto, Keanu Reeves seems to have pursued the normal interests of any school kid. Home in the afternoon, he'd stuff himself with peanut butter and crackers, before embarking on his paper route (later sold to a friend when the route was on its last legs) and sneaking into the local flea-pit cinema to watch a double bill of second-run Bruce Lee movies. When at home, he lavished his attentions on his bull mastiff, named Jupiter. All round, it was a good and fairly privileged life. After all, it was not everyone who could boast of having their photograph taken at age six by celebrity snapper Richard Avedon.

Before long Keanu had another father figure in his life – Patricia's third husband, Toronto rock promoter Robert Miller. Of all the men in his life to date, Miller was to stay the longest. During the five years he was part of the family, Miller added his own contribution – Karina, born when Keanu was twelve years old.

The Reeves family enjoyed a good standard of living in Toronto, a fact that Keanu was only really to appreciate years later. 'You won't find any stories of poverty or ghettos in this dude's closet. When I see stuff in Los Angeles now, I realise how safe and sheltered my upbringing was. It was a great place, no graffiti, cool people. The roughest it got was when we slung chestnuts at each other and built go-karts. I was a middle-class white boy with an absent father, a strong-willed mother, and two beautiful younger sisters,' said Keanu, defining himself and his family background.

For a while as a teenager, Keanu got seriously into the great Canadian sport of ice hockey. 'Keanu was major hockey,' recalled Paul Aaron in an interview in *Macleans.* 'That's all he talked about, thought about.' He and pal Evan Williams would play regularly, and Keanu began to harbour secret ambitions of pursuing the sport professionally. 'He was almost gangly, tall and thin, with long hair over his eyes,' remembered John O'Flaherty, his hockey coach at the time. 'He was always smiling, but I don't remember him ever being neat.'

'It's a thrilling game,' said Keanu of his hockey-playing days, when he was often the goalie and was so good at stopping the puck he was known simply as The Wall. 'Lots of drama, lots of physical contact. Stop the puck, keep the puck out of the net,' was Keanu's own recollection of his early sporting endeavours. Although he was not to follow up on his ice hockey interest professionally, it was to serve him well in one of his earliest film roles.

His nascent sporting ambition was soon discarded in favour of his 'thirrsst for the theeeatre', as Keanu mockingly called his acting interest. His stepfather Paul Aaron had stayed in touch with Keanu after leaving the family, and during school vacations Keanu would fly out to stay with him, often visiting the sets of whatever production he was working on. It was Keanu's first taste of real movie-making, spending time in Hollywood watching the production of films like *A Force of One*, *A Different Story* or NBC's Emmy-winning TV drama *The Miracle Worker*. These vacation experiences strengthened Keanu's ever-growing desire to pursue a serious acting career as soon as he possibly could.

At thirteen, just as his acting ambition was crystallising, Keanu saw his real father for the final time, before he was to be jailed. 'I knew him up until I was six, then I saw him occasionally when I would go to Hawaii on holidays. He taught me how to roller skate, we went hunting together and he taught me how to cook. He had a *je ne sais quoi* about his step. I remember being little and grabbing his finger; his hands seemed so big back then. The last time I saw him was when I was thirteen. It was at night and we were in Kauai. I remember him speaking about the stars. Something about the world is a box. And I looked up, and I had no clue what he was talking about. "No, Dad, the Earth is round. It's not a rectangle, man." I remember his speaking about the stars as we looked up.' After that visit, Samuel Nowlin Reeves vanished for ten years, staying out of contact with his family in Toronto.

'He never talked about his real dad,' remembered childhood friend Shawn Aberle. 'If he ever came up in conversation, Keanu would change the subject. There was a lot of love in the family, certainly from the female side. But from the male side, Keanu got much more of a tough love. He felt a little bit more alone.'

This loneliness was to haunt Keanu throughout his life. During his school years he would develop an anti-authoritarian streak which often got him into trouble with teachers and was even to result in him being thrown out of one school. Without a strong father figure to guide him, Keanu was to make up his own rules of behaviour.

For most of his childhood prior to his teenage years, Keanu had seen his loyalties divided between Samuel Reeves and Paul Aaron. His final separation from his real father was to cause Keanu to build up a fear of loss that would dominate his relationships in years to come. Unable to get close to anyone as he was forever anxious that they would eventually leave him, Keanu found his romantic life restricted and limited. His drive and ambition was to be channelled into his films instead. More immediately, the absence of his father was to show in Keanu's attitude to his schooling.

During Grades 9 and 10, when Keanu was aged between fourteen and fifteen he attended North Toronto Collegiate School, where some of his teachers noticed a vague sadness in him. 'I don't think he was a happy child here,' felt drama teacher Paul Robert. He felt Keanu was too independently minded to fit into the school's structured ways, and that clashes were inevitable.

To further his interest in acting, the teenage Keanu Reeves had begun drama classes and tried out at auditions for American TV shows and occasional movies shooting in Canada. At the same time, Keanu began having trouble at school. He went through four in quick succession, including Catholic boys' school De La Salle College, where he failed every class, with the exception of Latin. 'It was the only class that I liked. My attendance record was very bad. I was lazy. I knew I wanted to act when I was halfway through Grade 11, I guess, and school wasn't important.' Keanu clearly lacked any respect for authority during his later schooling. His inability to do as he was told was to result in early departures from several schools and to put his early acting opportunities under threat.

The one arena where Keanu could let go – other than the hockey rink – was drama class, where his teacher recalled him being head-and-shoulders above the other pupils. 'He wanted to push farther, to do some heavy duty role playing. But most students at that age didn't have the maturity to do it.'

Alternating between sport and theatre, Keanu stretched his mental and physical muscles. 'Even when he was tending goal,' recalled former coach Scott Barber, 'he would start reciting Shakespeare.' Keanu's year at the private De La Salle College saw him voted Most Valuable Player as goalie for the hockey team. Out of school, he continued his interest by working at a hockey rink, sharpening skates.

Work in a restaurant called Pastissima, where he made 100 pounds of pasta a day, helped Keanu's income. He was known to shut up the restaurant at odd times of the day and night in order to head off for acting auditions around Toronto. His boss didn't mind, though, as the good-looking teenager had a way with the customers. Although waiting on tables, Keanu would never miss the opportunity to put on a show, and his good-natured theatrical kidding proved a draw for customers.

He got his first taste of stage work at De La Salle College in a school production of Arthur Miller's *The Crucible*. Asking the question 'What am I?' on-stage, an appreciative female member of the audience was heard to mutter 'A hunk . . .' It was an early indication of the interest Keanu Reeves was to generate in some sections of his audiences.

To further his chances of gaining employment in theatre, Keanu enrolled in the newly opened Toronto High School for the Performing Arts, forsaking De La Salle for a more theatre-oriented education. There were 25 places available and all Keanu had to his credit was one appearance in *The Crucible*. He was up against other kids with much more professional theatre experience than himself. Surprising his mother – who had reluctantly given him permission to try out for the school – and himself, Keanu was offered a place. 'That became his sole abiding interest,' recalled Paul Aaron, as hockey fell a poor second in Keanu's interests. 'I mean, every part of it – the voice, the movement, the contemporary, the classic . . .'

Despite giving the school his all, Keanu was asked to leave, according to hockey pal Evan Williams, after a disagreement about dramatic technique with one of his teachers. To finish the 'discussion' the teacher told Keanu he'd just have to bite the bullet, to which the cocky youth replied: 'Yeah, but I don't have to eat the whole rifle!'

Keanu and canine friend relaxing together.

'I'm not very good with authority,' admitted Keanu later. 'When people in school kept trying to tell me what to do, it would infuriate me. When I don't feel free and can't do what I want, I just react. I go against it.'

His teen rebellion was limited – at sixteen Keanu had asked his mother's permission to become an actor – but he did have his moments. 'When I was seventeen, I had my first car, a 1969 122 Volvo. It was British racing green with bricks holding up the front seat, and a good stereo. I remember being with some friends and driving that car from Toronto to Buffalo to see the Ramones and that was very adventurous. There was a punk rock girl in the back seat with a racoon on her shoulder and the Clash was playing loud, and all these questions were running through my head: would we make it? We're under-age, can we get in? You know, drinking and watching the Ramones. It was such a good time.'

While he appreciated the good times being a teenager, Keanu knew he would have to work at it if he was serious about becoming an actor. Going back to school and taking serious classes seemed to be the only way forward for him. 'That didn't really happen until I was seventeen or eighteen,' he admitted. 'I started taking acting courses at night. It just seemed the thing to do. Most of it was out of respect for acting. I worked at some Stanislavsky stuff and I was playing around with sense memory. I got started crashing auditions and then I got some jobs and joined the community theatre.'

By 1983, aged nineteen and thrown out of his first acting school, Keanu Reeves decided to give achieving his ambition one last shot. Every Sunday he would attend a community theatre school called Leah Posluns. He was not the best potential actor the school had enrolled, but director Rose Dubin was impressed by the Shakespeare soliloquy he performed during his try-out. The same could not be said for the judges at the Stratford Festival in Ontario, who were less than impressed, twice rejecting his applications to join their summer Shakespeare troupe. Not to be stopped, Keanu spent the summer – in his first real trip alone away from home – at the Hedgerow Theatre in Pennsylvania, studying under Jasper Deeter. At the time, Keanu was definitely fixated on Shakespeare as the essence of true drama, and was pursuing acting as a means of getting on stage. Movies were not high on the young would-be actor's agenda. He wanted to be a 'proper' actor.

'To perform Shakespeare you get to say very profound words and in the body it feels more thrilling. Your spirit, your intellect, your heart and your voice all have to, at a very high degree, melt into the speaking of words and behaviour. For me all of these things are missing in action pictures. In Shakespeare, it's pure.' Keanu retained his teenage infatuation with the words and emotions of the Bard, it being influential in his later performances in *My Own Private Idaho* (loosely based by director Gus Van Sant on *Henry IV*), Kenneth Branagh's *Much Ado About Nothing* and his run on stage in Winnipeg playing the title character in *Hamlet*.

Keanu's attendance at Leah Posluns was to lead to his first genuine stage experience outside of school plays. He struck up a friendship with another wannabe young actor, Alan Powell, who found that beyond a certain point Keanu wouldn't even let friends get to know him. 'We'd play off each other,' said Powell, of co-starring with Keanu in school workshop productions. 'The chemistry was dynamic. He was the friend I'd never had as a child. But he was a secretive guy about his life. You could be hanging with the guy for three years; suddenly he'd introduce you to someone who turned out to be a friend of his all that time. You could never get close to the guy.'

Keanu did value his work with Powell – the practice led to him winning through an audition and scoring his first legitimate theatre role in 1984's *Wolfboy*. This homoerotic theatrical oddity, written by Brad Fraser and staged at Toronto's Passe Muraille Theatre, had Keanu cast as a young innocent placed in a psychiatric hospital, only to be set upon by a deranged boy who believes he's a werewolf. He almost didn't get the part, failing to impress director John Palmer. 'His diction was a mess,' said Palmer. 'He would skip words and say lines like he was trying to figure out what they meant.'

However, there was a star quality about Keanu even then, something that caught Palmer's attention. He called it an energy and a glow. 'I didn't want professional actors, so I advertised in the personals. I got totally fucked-up hustlers – and Keanu.'

In what was to be the beginning of the 'Is Keanu Gay?' question that was to dog the rest of his career, *Wolfboy* played largely to Toronto's gay community. 'You get this innocent kid,' said Palmer, 'one of the most gorgeous kids anyone's ever seen, in white shorts – and we oiled them . . . what do you want for ten bucks?'

Co-starring with Keanu was Carl Marotte, playing the street hustler who befriends and then kills Keanu's character with a sensual bite to the neck (shades of his later experience in *Bram Stoker's Dracula*). Marotte claimed he and Keanu took the play's homoerotic undertones in their strides, but did struggle when asked to become more explicit for a series of still photographs being shot to promote the play. 'We asked them to test the boundaries,' admitted photographer David

'Testing the boundaries': Keanu and his Wolfboy *co-star Carl Marotte.*

Hlynsky, who sprayed the pair of bare-chested stars with water for the required 'sweaty glow'. Hlynsky suggested the actors should kiss and caress each other. 'They were both apprehensive about it, but they understood the sexual tension in the parts they were playing.' Hlynsky was around Keanu a lot during this 'gay' period and couldn't help but notice his attraction for both sexes. He definitely saw in Keanu a connection with another young star of the past. 'Keanu had a James Dean charisma,' asserted the photographer, whose early pictures captured some of Keanu's developing star power. 'He's a beautiful man in an androgynous way. The Toronto gay community was turned on by Keanu and still is. I know he and his mother were very happy with the pictures, because she told me so.'

How to capitalise on his sex appeal, to both men and women, was something that Keanu was to learn very early on in his acting career and use to great advantage much later. A friend suggested that, whatever he said later, at the time he enjoyed his *Wolfboy* experience. 'He had no qualms about the play . . . in fact, he was very enthusiastic because it was so offbeat and shocking.' *Wolfboy* was a big hit in Toronto's gay community, and proved to be a good calling card for Keanu – although later on when mainstream stardom beckoned, all memory of the play would be expunged from his official list of credits.

The role won the aspiring actor his first Equity card – and his first bad reviews. Although the gay community loved the play, mainstream Toronto critics were not as impressed. In April 1984 the *Toronto Globe and Mail* dubbed the play 'a real howler', while the *Toronto Sun* went for the obvious headline: 'Bloody Awful: Awful Bloody'. The paper awarded the company's efforts its lowest critical rating – one star. However, neither Keanu nor John Palmer was particularly put out by this savaging at the hands of the critics – they knew who their audience were and they were coming to the theatre in droves.

While at Leah Posluns, Keanu scored his first professional television credit. 'The first professional role that I got was on a Canadian show called *Hangin' In*. It's about a youth counselling centre. I was really lucky to get on it – lots of Canadian actors get their lucky breaks on it.' Although he had only one line in what amounted to little more than a bit part on the show, it was a beginning for Keanu. He saw it as leading directly onto other work. '*Hangin' In* is a godsend for young actors in Toronto . . . They give lots of roles out to young kids. It was a three-camera shoot, and I played a tough street kid. I wore stupid clothes and had no idea of what I was doing. My line was, "Hey lady, can I use the shower?"'

The appearance in *Hangin' In* did lead to further work for the actor, as well as to an agent – Tracy Moore at Noble Talent. Using a shower was her first piece of advice to the wannabe actor. Keanu had a habit of putting personal hygiene way down on his list of priorities, such were his scatterbrained ways. 'We didn't want him to be remembered as a smelly, sloppy kid,' recalled Moore of her new client. 'His attitude was that didn't have anything to do with his acting ability.'

Keanu did more community theatre, and a couple of TV shows, *Night Heat* (as 'Thug 1') and *The Comedy Factory*, as well as one-shot TV commercials, one for Coca Cola and one for Kellogg's Corn Flakes breakfast cereal. 'I once did an advert for Kellogg's that got me loads of money. I didn't put it in the bank, I just put it in a basket and dipped into it when I needed it. Now I pay very careful attention to everything – well, my accountant does,' said Keanu of his early adventures in advertising.

The actor's first real big break also came from another Leah Posluns connection –

this time to Hollywood rather than theatre. Movie director Steven Stern had links with the school through his sister, and he had Keanu audition for a part in a TV movie entitled *Young Again* which he was due to shoot. 'There was something about him I liked as a person. Funny, yet a serious side. I told him to take the script home and read it for the lead,' recalled Stern.

Back at Disney, the studio employing Stern, executives were incredulous that he was considering an unknown for the lead role. Stern personally paid for Keanu to fly to Los Angeles for a screen test, and he persuaded then-Disney executives Michael Eisner and Jeffrey Katzenberger to view it. After his audition, with his hopes riding high as he waited to hear the outcome, it was back to trying for bit parts in movies shot locally in Toronto by visiting Hollywood companies.

For all his serious study, community theatre work and minor appearances in TV movies, it was to be his prior interest in the sport of ice hockey that was to lead to Keanu Reeves making his feature film debut in the Patrick Swayze–Rob Lowe starring film *Youngblood* (1986). With the director looking for Toronto locals who could play ice hockey and had some acting experience, the film was a natural vehicle for Keanu. When he heard from both his hockey and acting class sources that a new film was shooting in town, he couldn't wait to become involved. During an eight-week training period for the two main stars – Lowe and Swayze – Keanu auditioned and won a role in the film in July 1984, just two months before his twentieth birthday. It was a dream come true and the combination of the young man's two main interests in life.

The film came from the real-life experiences of writer-director Peter Markle, who'd scored with the hit ski comedy *Hot Dog: The Movie* in 1984. Rob Lowe featured in the film as Dean Youngblood, a talented young skater who has left his home behind for a career in ice hockey. In tow is Jessie (Cynthia Gibb), a young hockey fan and daughter of the team coach attracted to the game for its fierce, violent competition. Also on the scene is Derek (Swayze), a veteran of the amateur leagues, on the verge of a professional career – until he's assaulted by a savage opponent in the final moments of a critical game. Swayze's nemesis is Racki (George Finn), the most fearsome player on the ice, and his next target is Dean Youngblood.

Teetering precariously close to teen soap opera, the drama of *Youngblood* was an indication of the films in which Keanu would find himself in the near future. Although in only a minor role here, he was nonetheless beginning to fulfil the 'distressed teen' roles that he would play right up to his career-defining character in *Bill and Ted's Excellent Adventure*. He doesn't appear until twenty minutes into the film, but thereafter he's featured in the hockey games as the goalie, albeit hidden behind his hockey mask. He's a featured team player in training sessions, the usual clichéd dressing room scenes and in the on-ice antics and confrontations. His performance consists of unintelligible mutterings in a bizarre accent, and bemused looks (later to be perfected in *Bill and Ted's Excellent Adventure*). He shows little signs of his soon-to-be-developed star power and doesn't share much screen-time with Patrick Swayze, his future *Point Break* co-star. Although Keanu is not featured heavily in *Youngblood*, he pops up now and again as the film focuses on Lowe and Swayze, two top '80s idols whom Keanu Reeves would later eclipse in star status. It was to be a long climb from twelfth billing in the cast list (as 'K.C. Reeves') to being billed above the title.

Determined to capture the visceral excitement of the game for the cinema audience, Markle decided that he would treat the camera as a player during the ice hockey sequences and have it following the player's complex moves around the ice. Avoiding all the high-tech suggestions as to how to achieve this result, Markle went for the simple approach. So it was that Keanu Reeves found himself kitted out in hockey gear on the ice, being chased around by a film cameraman firmly strapped into a wheelchair. 'Without any refinements, the wheelchair showed us just how fast and fluid we could get,' admitted director of photography Mark Irwin.

The film was praised by *Variety*, with the wheelchair camerawork coming in for special praise, but the film debut of Keanu Reeves was not noted: 'Scenes on the ice look great, and Lowe truly looks like the fast and accurate son-of-a-gun he's supposed to be.' The film received a mixed reception from British critics, for whom the subject matter and milieu were somewhat more exotic and unusual. The *Daily Mail* raved about *Youngblood* as 'a taut, gritty and involving piece of cinema, brought to nerve-tingling excitement by superb camerawork and editing'.

By October 1984, Keanu was pleased to find that as a result of *Youngblood* he'd secured a second film-acting role in another sporting film. *Flying,* which was released in some territories under the title *Dream to Believe*, was a feel-good movie that owed much to the plot of *Flashdance*. Olivia D'Abo played the lead part of a young gymnast who has to overcome a traumatic leg injury before she can go on to win a sought-after medal. Sixties British film star Rita Tushingham appeared as her tough-but-loving coach, almost unrecognisable in a ginger fright-wig. Also in the cast was a young Jessica Steen, later to make her mark in sci-fi TV shows like *Babylon 5* creator

Keanu managed to combine his love of hockey and acting in his feature film debut Youngblood.

J. Michael Strazynski's *Captain Power* and Steven Spielberg's doomed *Earth 2*.

Keanu was among several local actors who won roles in this Canadian production. He played Tommy, an eccentric school friend of D'Abo who admired her from afar. Director Paul Lynch was torn in his choice between Keanu and another promising young actor, but in the end Keanu's clearly developing abilities secured him the role. A minor role in his acting credits, *Flying* is the film in which he played someone closest to his off-screen self. His genuineness, though, wasn't enough to win over critics when the film secured a belated release in December 1986.

Variety berated the film as being deserving of 'little attention', but it did gain significant notices in the local Toronto papers. 'Reeves and D'Abo . . . show a touch of insouciance' according to the *Toronto Globe and Mail*. Keanu's attempts, however, did win over some critics, with the *Toronto Sun* calling the young actor 'quirky', while the *Toronto Star* claimed the young actor had managed to breathe life into his character.

By the spring of 1985, Keanu was back on stage, playing his first Shakespearean role. He won the part of Mercutio in *Romeo and Juliet*, staged by the senior students of Leah Posluns. The director was Lewis Baumander, artistic director of the Skylight Theatre. Baumander was impressed by the fact that Keanu came to the open auditions with the notion in mind of playing a particular part. In his experience, most students were desperate to get any part. The play ran for only a single week, from 28 May to 2 June, but Keanu gave his all to the performance. This performance stayed with Keanu, firing his ambitions to play more Shakespeare, preferably on stage. It stayed with Baumander, too, who was later to re-team with Keanu, when he had won fame as a movie star, to stage a stage production of *Hamlet*, with the actor playing the title role, in Winnipeg, Canada.

His debut films may not have set the box office alight, but greater opportunities waited just around the corner for twenty-year-old Keanu Reeves. He was overjoyed to learn from Steven Stern that he'd won the title role in the Disney TV movie *Young Again*. This was to be his big opportunity – a chance to relocate to Hollywood, where the young actor knew he had to be to realise his growing ambitions.

CHAPTER TWO

Teen on the Edge

B Y THE EARLY SUMMER of 1985 the twenty-year-old Keanu Reeves was ready to capitalise on his local Toronto triumphs – his stage work in *Wolfboy* and appearances in TV bit parts, as well as his feature film debut in *Youngblood*. He was ready to leave home and move to Los Angeles to pursue a serious Hollywood film career. Winning the part in *Young Again* was the ideal reason for finally leaving home to pursue his career.

It was a pivotal time in his life. Although his trip to Pennsylvania had taken him away from home, the longest Keanu had been living away from his family had been several weeks camped out in a friend's basement while his mother renovated the house. It was clear to him, though, that he could do little more in Toronto to further his career. Parts would, of course, be much more available in Los Angeles than they had been back in Canada, when Keanu had to wait for visiting projects filming on location, or rare local productions, before he even got a shot at an audition. It was time to put the schooling and classes behind him and move his professional life on.

'I was at a point where I had done the most I could do in Toronto. I was tired of playing the best friend, thug number one and the tall guy,' said Keanu. 'I got into my dumpy 1969 Volvo and drove here with $3,000. I stayed at my stepfather's and proceeded to go into the darkness that is LA.'

It was natural that, upon arriving in LA looking for work, it was to Paul Aaron the young actor would turn. It also meant he could let Aaron know about his mother Patricia's latest marriage, to fourth husband – hairdresser Jack Bond. Aaron's advice to his stepson had been carefully parcelled out through the years. He didn't want to be seen to be pushing the young man into an acting career, but neither did he wish to stifle Keanu's developing ambitions. Offering house room to Keanu was one way of ensuring that he had a decent start upon arrival in LA. Aaron was to play a more decisive and long-running role in Keanu's professional life, by suggesting that the would-be actor see Erwin Stoff, who in the mid-'80s was just setting himself up as a Hollywood talent manager.

Stoff was to develop over the years from 1986 into an old-fashioned talent manager, one who devotes his attentions to a handful of specific clients. His 3 Arts Entertainment company was in the forefront of a late '80s resurgence in management companies.

'Agents look at themselves as covering the marketplace,' warned the bearded, balding Stoff. 'We look at ourselves as covering the client.' Whereas agents at big agencies tend to handle around 60 clients each, at 3 Arts each rep focused on about fifteen key people and became more involved in career management than individual film deals. Separate agents would handle those deals.

Keanu was convinced and signed on with Stoff, who worked quickly and found him a traditional Hollywood agent in the shape of Hildy Gottlieb Hill, then head of talent at the International Creative Management (ICM) Agency. 'In twenty minutes I was crazy about him. He was very fresh,' recalled Hill of her first meeting with Keanu Reeves. After the actor had left, Hill boasted to a colleague: 'I've just signed a new client, and I don't even know if he can act . . .' It was to be a question audiences and critics would be asking about Keanu Reeves throughout most of his career – can he really act?

Such concerns were not at the forefront of Keanu's mind. He just moved out of Paul Aaron's rented home into an apartment of his own on the corner of Fairfax and Beverly. He was where he wanted to be – in Hollywood, signed with a manager and an agent – and he had the title role in the Disney TV movie *Young Again*.

The story had 40-year-old Robert Urich wishing to be young again – and magically turning into Keanu Reeves. As the young Urich, Keanu goes skateboarding, disco dancing and visiting malls. Returning to school, though, the older Urich in the younger Keanu body felt terribly out of place. The role won Keanu a rave review from *Variety* after its May 1986 TV screening. 'Reeves steps in with terrific success as Urich the youth. . . Reeves's open-faced, exuberant study of the boy who turns into a young man in love goes a long way towards keeping the fantasy in the realm of reality.'

Now all he needed was a stand-out role, one that would make Hollywood sit up and take notice of the new arrival. It wasn't to happen immediately, but before the year was out, Keanu Reeves would have made the film that marked him out as a talent to be watched closely. He was a picky newcomer, too, apparently turning down the lead role in *Platoon* as because he objected to the violence and guns, according to director Oliver Stone. 'He was a bit of a pacifist at the time,' claimed Stone, '. . .had a real thing about guns.'

It was an opportunity missed, but a sign of some of the eccentricities to come in Keanu's selection of roles. *Platoon* went on to win four Oscars, including one for Best Picture. The lead part was played by Charlie Sheen, who was nominated for Best Actor. Although Sheen pipped Keanu to the role at this early stage in the actor's career, he was later to be envious of Keanu's more consistent successes, as he told *Movieline* magazine. 'Emilio [Estevez, Sheen's actor brother] and I sit around scratching our fucking heads, thinking, "How did this guy get in?" I mean – how does Keanu work with Coppola and Bertolucci and I don't get a shot at that?'

Keanu was to look back on his beginnings in Hollywood, and consider how his approach to his career had changed: 'I jumped into acting without an ultimate goal, and it's just recently that I've realised that I don't have any goals. In the immediacy of being in Hollywood, now in my life as it is, I would like to play a very neurotic, crazy, preferably mean, evil character. Most of the characters I've played so far have been good people; they all, in a sense, are in possession of sort of a naiveté. I guess that's me, and I'd like to explore and exploit some other stuff.'

Keanu was spot-on in analysing his own typecasting. Although he was twenty when he arrived in Los Angeles, his baby-faced good looks resulted in years of casting as teen high-schoolers with problems – a role he was overly familiar with from his own real life experiences in Canadian high schools.

Earning his Screen Actors Guild union card became a first priority for Keanu, and winning a role in the 1986 TV movie *Under the Influence* was his ticket to union membership, even if that particular film had its drawbacks, such as reporting to the set at 8 a.m. every morning. 'I thought this was . . . unfair,' admitted Keanu. 'It's hard to act in the morning. The muse isn't even awake . . .'

Starring in the above-average TV movie was Andy Griffith as family man Noah Talbot, who refuses to acknowledge he's an alcoholic. Keanu featured alongside Joyce Van Patten, William Schallert and Season Hubley, under the early morning direction of Thomas Carter. The movie had been written by recovering alcoholic Joyce Reberta-Burditt, drawing on her own experiences to produce an incisive script that delivered a powerful message.

Keanu was cast in the role of Eddie, the second son in the family after Stephen (stand-up comedian Paul Provenza), who has turned his family experiences into routines he performs on stage. Keanu's character of Eddie does not have that escape option and so hopes to both impress his father and rebel against him by becoming like him, by drinking and risking the dangers of alcoholism himself.

Of Keanu's very early performances prior to *River's Edge*, *Under the Influence* was the most accomplished. Although part of a large ensemble cast, Keanu more than held his own against the TV veteran Andy Griffith. More importantly, in the loathing of his fictional father, Keanu seemed to bring out something of his own hatred for Samuel, the father who had abandoned him. And as his character drifted to becoming an alcoholic like his fictional father in *Under the Influence*, Keanu found echoes of his own fear that he would turn out to be an addictive personality like his drug-addicted real-life father and abandon his relationships. It was to be a fear which would prevent the actor from pursuing any serious personal relationships in his life, but also one that would spur him on to his successes in Hollywood.

As Keanu settled into life in Los Angeles, more work followed *Under the Influence*. In the Home Box Office effort *Act of Vengeance* (1986) he played opposite Charles Bronson as a 'psychotic assassin' (foreshadowing his later comedy role in Lawrence Kasdan's *I Love You to Death*). The John Mackenzie-directed TV movie was based on a true story and had Bronson (minus his trademark moustache) as a union member whose challenge for the leadership leads to his family's murder. Young novice Keanu was in good company, as the film also featured Ellen Barkin, Wilford Brimley and Ellen Burstyn.

John Mackenzie recalled Keanu as being difficult to work with, although the problems seem mainly to have stemmed from the young actor's inexperience of movie sets and the process of film-making. Mackenzie had cast Keanu in the role as he saw something 'off-the-wall' in the actor's own personality. He wasn't too pleased, however, when this very quality came across during Keanu's work on the film. He was clumsy during scenes and annoying to Mackenzie, who called the actor 'an upstart'. Speculating that Keanu's behaviour may have been down to drug-taking, Mackenzie set things right by giving the actor a severe dressing down. It was an approach that worked, and he was to watch his Ps and Qs for the rest of the shoot. It was the first, but not the last time that Keanu was to be perceived as 'difficult' by one of his directors.

Finding himself constantly busy on films, Keanu had little time to pursue a life away from movie sets. *Act of Vengeance* was followed up with a leading role in *The Brotherhood of Justice*, another TV movie with a message. Keanu played Derick, a rich kid on the make who drives around in a flashy red sports car and has no problem drawing a group of girls around himself, an attraction no doubt helped by his captaincy of the football team. It was the ideal teen role for Keanu, a chance for him to stretch his wings by taking on a more central part in a drama. He was also playing a bad guy, as his seemingly all-American kid becomes the head of a vigilante gang that starts off meaning well but quickly gets out of control. Kiefer Sutherland played the high school do-gooder with whom Keanu's over-the-edge character clashed.

With both *Variety* and the *Los Angeles Times* having commended the young actor's performance in *Under the Influence*, reaction to *The Brotherhood of Justice* came as something of a disappointment. The *Los Angeles Times* was particularly unimpressed, pointing out that as Keanu's eventual doubt about the gang's activities 'weighs less heavily on him than the distress of losing his girlfriend, it hardly makes for compelling viewing'. As he continued the rounds of auditions, he won more teens in the family roles in TV movies-of-the-week like *Moving Day*, made as part of the *Trying Times* teen series for the PBS network.

Despite his work rate, it was pointed out to Keanu by his managers that his unusual name was in fact getting in the way of him winning roles. 'That was a terrible, terrible phase that lasted about a month,' recalled Keanu about his brief flirtation with changing his unusual, but real, name to something more 'Hollywood'. 'I was informed that my manager and my agent at the time were having trouble getting me in to see some casting agents because of my name. It had an ethnicity to it that they found was getting in the way. And so they said I had to change my name. That freaked me out completely. I came up with names like Page Templeton III. And Chuck Spidina, from my middle name, Charles. Eventually they picked K.C. Reeves. Ugh, terrible. When I would go to auditions, I'd tell them my name was Keanu anyway.'

William Goldman once claimed that no one in Hollywood knows anything, and it is ironic to note that while the feature film industry recognised in Keanu Reeves's almost ethnic, vaguely Chinese or Asian good looks a star in the making, his name on its own served to block him from roles, for the very same racial reasons. The concern of his managers was apparently misplaced, as Keanu he was to stay.

As a jobbing actor, Keanu found many scripts coming his way and opportunities for auditions before him, but as the new kid on the block he had to resist the strong temptation to be too picky about what he chose to do. 'I want to be enlightened, dude,' he claimed. 'I [want to do] interesting stories, interesting people, character development, ideas being posed, clash/conflicts, hate, love, war, death, success, fame, failure, redemption, salvation, death, hell, sin, good food, bad food, nice smells, colours and big tits.'

Some, but not all, of those elements were to be found when he co-starred with a young Drew Barrymore in *Babes in Toyland*, an ill-advised and overlong TV version of the Victor Herbert operetta, which featured a new score by Leslie Bricusse. Directed by Clive Donner and clocking in at slightly over two and a half hours, *Babes in Toyland* retained only *Toyland* and *March of the Wooden Soldiers* from the original score to punctuate the screenplay by Pulitzer prizewinner Paul Zindel. Also in the cast were Richard Mulligan and Pat Morita (later to feature in *Even Cowgirls Get the Blues*).

Keanu co-starred with Lori Loughlin (centre) and Kiefer Sutherland (right)
in the TV movie Brotherhood of Justice.

The TV movie did give Keanu his first film-related trip abroad, to the Bavaria Studios in Munich, Germany in July 1986. The tight, 33-day shoot was simply not enough time for director Donner to do justice to the source material, and the finished broadcast version showed every sign of having been a rushed job. Keanu played the boyfriend of Barrymore's older sister in the real world, and Jack Nimble in the fantasy land into which Barrymore finds herself pitched. With Barrymore in tow he endeavours to overthrow the evil Barnaby Barnacle who plans to take over Toyland. The key to defeating the evil villain was to have Barrymore reaffirm her belief in the fantasy of toys and make-believe. Dancing and singing, Keanu made the best of a difficult part.

Broadcast just before Christmas in the United States, critics leapt upon the production's inadequacies with a vengeance. The *New York Times* accused the cast of being on 'automatic pilot', while *USA Today* simply described *Babes in Toyland* as 'painful to behold'. Luckily enough, none of the criticism stuck to Keanu.

There was one personal benefit for Keanu in taking on the role in *Babes in Toyland*. He enjoyed his first film-set affair with co-star Jill Schoelen, who played his on-screen girlfriend. The brief affair seems to have been treated almost as a holiday romance by Keanu. Schoelen, however, seems to have made a habit of serious involvements with her co-stars. A year later, while making the 1987 horror-comedy *Cutting Class*, Schoelen was to enjoy a three-month liaison with rising heart-throb Brad Pitt.

As his work increased in frequency, Keanu found that getting into and out of the parts he played became second nature, even if there was a minor downside. 'The first two weeks after I've wrapped a movie, I'm out in space,' he said. 'I can't speak about anything.'

All this work, even if much of it was in second string roles as the boy-next-door, or as a family member only ever seen at the breakfast table, was great experience for Keanu. He realised he was on a learning curve and used this period of his career to his best advantage, managing to sample a variety of teen roles, still playing on screen well under his actual age of 22 years.

'All I can say is that I try to give and I try to learn,' said Keanu of his approach to these early roles. Asked in an interview about the best aspects of fame, he was nothing if not realistic about his status in 1986 in a Hollywood crowded out with would-be hot young actors. 'I almost said chicks and sex and fucking and money – but that hasn't happened yet. What do I like most about being an actor? Acting! The best thing for me about being an actor is acting. I mean, what else is there?'

'What else is there' was also a question to be asked about the young actor's off-screen life. Although extremely busy as a jobbing actor making his way in Hollywood, Keanu was also trying to fit into the social life of LA. Having set up in his own apartment, Keanu was finding his feet in a city that he didn't know very well, but did soon feel at home in. With his first income from his handful of movie roles, Keanu had switched his Volvo for a motorbike, and he took to exploring the hills of LA, sometimes late at night. Having left school far behind, Keanu took up reading as a hobby, turning his attention to anything from popular fiction to classics of literature or scientific textbooks. When not acting, he made a point of trying to keep his mind busy by sticking his head in a book and absorbing the knowledge he'd missed during his years of playing up at school.

Mean and moody: in River's Edge *Keanu played a darker teen rebel.*

Everything was about to change for Keanu when he won the role of a seriously troubled teen in *River's Edge*.

Based on a shocking true story which took place in Milpitas, California in 1981, *River's Edge* was the first significant scriptwriting work by disabled writer-director Neal Jimenez, later to make his mark with *The Waterdance* (1992). The story of the rape and murder of fourteen-year-old Marcy Conrad on a seeming whim by her sixteen-year-old boyfriend Jacques Broussard fascinated Jimenez, who was then a film student in San Jose. He used the story of Broussard bragging to his friends and displaying the corpse to them as the basis of a set project for his screenwriting class. Although his script was not welcomed by his tutor, who felt it was too dark, it did spark interest among the studios. After consideration, though, most backed away from the obviously bleak subject matter, seeing it as being too controversial for a mainstream film. Jimenez's saviours came in the form of British film company Hemdale, behind the financing of such controversial American films as *Platoon*, *At Close Range* and *Salvador*, who soon had the project in production as a low budget film to be directed by Tim Hunter.

The film opens in the aftermath of the murder, as teenager Samson smokes a joint next to the naked dead body of his girlfriend, Marcy. Unknown to Samson, he's been seen, by Tim, the twelve-year-old brother of Samson's pal Matt (Keanu Reeves). Getting involved with the older boys, Tim is soon introduced to Feck, the boy's one-legged, ex-biker drug supplier (played by '60s icon Dennis Hopper). The story of Samson's actions soon spreads throughout the school as pupils trek to the river's edge to see the body over several days, without going to the authorities. As the repercussions spread, Matt eventually decides he has to inform the police, but they can't prevent Feck from visiting his own brand of eye-for-an-eye justice on the amoral killer Samson.

Hunter chose an eclectic cast to bring the bleak tale to life. Switched from sunny California to America's cold Midwest, Hunter ensured that the setting matched the subject matter. He wanted to do the same with the casting. He signed up Dennis Hopper, who was then in a rut in his career for the character role of Feck, and eccentric rising actor Crispin Glover (*Back to the Future*) as a key gang member. Keanu Reeves was cast as the only character in the film who begins to see the fact that the activities of the teenagers are wrong, and he finally admits all to the authorities.

Director Tim Hunter tackled this $1.7 million budget project almost as an anti-teen movie, certainly an anti-John Hughes movie. Hughes had made something of a name for himself writing and directing a series of feel-good teen movies starring the so-called brat pack, including such films as *The Breakfast Club* (which Keanu had auditioned for, but failed to win a part in), *Ferris Bueller's Day Off* and *St Elmo's Fire*. Splicing '60s values, through the Dennis Hopper character, with '80s nihilism, Hunter called the film 'a combination of the mundane and the surreal. That makes it an unusually tough film to get a handle on and watch from a comfortable perspective.'

Although not altogether happy with his work, Hunter was pleased to have been able to take a different perspective on the clichéd genre of the teen flick. 'River's Edge is far from perfect. In some ways it isn't even successful. But what I like about it is that so many teen movies that are social-issue oriented tend to skirt their own issues. Whereas these kids are dealing with the implications of this event from the minute they see the body, and they never get away from it. There's no bullshit – they're working it out through this picture.'

At the river's edge: Keanu and his co-stars contemplate their seemingly bleak future.

Ahead of its time in its nihilistic bleakness and refusal to conform to Hollywood's desire for happy endings, *River's Edge* failed to set the American box office on fire. After previews in Seattle in October 1986, the film gained good reviews from critics, but failed to draw in audiences. With Hemdale in financial difficulties, it was left to film festivals in Europe to promote the unusual project to potential audiences.

Of the critics writing about the film, Vincent Canby in the *New York Times* was the most positive about *River's Edge*, singling out the character of Matt, as played by Keanu Reeves. '*River's Edge* is the year's most riveting, most frightening horror film . . . To the extent that *River's Edge* has a sympathetic character, he's Matt (Keanu), the young man who finally does call the police, but who, when asked to explain why it took him so long, is genuinely baffled. "I don't know," he says. The unbelieving cop asks him what he felt when he saw the body of the girl, someone he'd known since grade school. Matt, furrowing his brow, replies, "Nothing."'

Richard Schickel, writing in *Time*, also saw Keanu's Matt as central to the film. 'Matt, who is played with exemplary restraint by Keanu Reeves, does finally violate their conspiracy and makes a tentative connection with traditional morality. But by this time the cold of this brave and singular work has seeped into our bones, we know that Matt is the exception to a bleak and deeply disturbing vision of adolescent life.'

Fans of Keanu may have noted the strong connection between Keanu's real life as a decent kid without a father and this role. David Denby in *New York* magazine wrote: 'The one who finally breaks away and goes to the cops, Matt (Keanu Reeves), is a decent boy struggling for clarity. Like the others, Matt lives in a squalid,

Keanu and Ione Skye Leitch in River's Edge.

trailer-trash house, with harassed, overworked adults. His own father had vanished, replaced by a noisy, exasperated lout; his mom, a nurse, is worn out. All the kids have grown up in a vacuum, without any models, any authority they can respect.'

Indeed, it was only later that *River's Edge* would really find its audience on video, becoming something of a celebrated cult movie in the process. Audiences may not have seen the film on its first release, but movie directors who were later to work with Keanu Reeves were to cite *River's Edge* as the first film which had brought the young actor to their attentions. He'd finally made it in Hollywood, even if he'd not yet clicked with movie audiences.

Some kids were deeply affected by Keanu's performance as Matt, as he recalled: 'Only one really heavy thing has happened to me. Once I met a kid who was seventeen and he dressed up like Matt, my character in *River's Edge*. He told me I was his idol, and he gave me loads of free food from the restaurant where he worked.'

Keanu himself seemed to realise that he was on the road to success, and he began to worry about its potential effects on him. In an early interview he connected his increasing visibility with his possible religious beliefs. 'I seem to pay some petty respect [to God] whenever I talk about my success. I talk about my fear of retribution for my success – that I must pay for it. I guess in some sort of deep-rooted way, I feel I haven't. I guess I'm paying tribute to irony. Irony can make you bitter, but, yeah, I guess I believe in God. No, I don't believe in God. I don't know. These things are still in turmoil.'

Partly through failing to win a part in 'brat pack' movie *The Breakfast Club*, Keanu Reeves had narrowly escaped being lumped in with that infamous group of young '80s actors which included Andrew McCarthy, Rob Lowe, Demi Moore, Emilio Estevez, Molly Ringwald and Ally Sheedy. It was something he was grateful for, eventually. He was glad he wasn't part of an identifiable trend in young Hollywood actors.

'This is what I feel is happening with actors in Hollywood,' explained Keanu. 'A lot of people I've been working with have a sense of darkness and seriousness about their point of view of acting. I think there are a lot of heavy actors who are going to come out and surprise people. They are going to help Hollywood. They are very sincere and generally well-read and smart about what they are doing. They have a strong point of view about their acting and their place in the world. We are getting more theatrical in our acting styles. Film in that sense is taking more risks. Even the actors who aren't doing anything yet but being cute and themselves will, hopefully, in the future push and expand their limits. We hope – because I'd like to spend six bucks and feel it was worth it.

'I'm not Dennis Hopper; I'm just doing what I'm doing – trying, at least. I'm trying to pursue what I'm curious about, trying to survive, and hopefully not be fucked up the ass by irony and the gods.'

Deciding where his ambition lay, Keanu had a hankering to make a bizarre, off-the-wall comedy. 'People are bored with being so literal. We need some more of that good old thirties, forties and fifties surrealism again, especially in our comedy. Audiences are ready to see more intelligent work.' Before that, though, Keanu had more teenage roles awaiting him, although he was now in his mid-twenties. He also had his first costume drama to tackle, as well as a near-fatal motorcycle accident that almost stopped his film career in its tracks.

CHAPTER THREE

Prince of Hollywood

NOW FIRMLY established in Hollywood after the critical reaction to his performance in *River's Edge*, Keanu Reeves was first choice for leading roles in teen movies with an edge or a difference. He'd marked himself out from the brat pack squad as a young actor more willing to stretch himself in his teen roles, even though he was now coming up to 24 years of age.

Indeed, it was another teen movie with a difference that gave Keanu one of his earliest top billing roles in 1988. Director Marisa Silver (daughter of Joan Micklin Silver, director of *Crossing Delancey*) and producer Frank Mancuso Jr planned *Permanent Record* as a youth movie with a more serious edge. 'Our purpose was to make an honest, dramatic movie, with young people in the leads,' said Mancuso Jr. 'In everyone's life something happens that changes you, you know from that moment on your life will never be the same again.'

The momentous event in *Permanent Record* is the suicide of a popular and musically talented high-schooler on the verge of graduation, and the effect his death has on the friends left behind to cope with their grief. Alan Boyce took the second billed role of David Sinclair, while Keanu Reeves carried the bulk of the film as Chris Townsend, the best friend who witnessed the suicide and then resents being left behind.

As the most popular student of Thurber High School, David Sinclair has it all – the sexy girlfriend (Pamela Gidley), the perfect mom (Kathy Baker), the car, and the band on the verge of a major recording session. The night he and Chris throw the biggest party of the year, David vanishes over a cliff edge. Everyone believes his death to be an accident, until Chris receives a suicide note in the post from David. It is then that the pupils, parents and school have to come to terms with the suicide.

What could have been a dark film turns out to be something of an uplifting experience, and much of its success has to do with how well Keanu manages to carry off the tough emotional scenes he has to deal with. For the first twenty minutes or so, he's the usual high-schooler he had played over and over again during this period – almost a first draft of Ted Logan, a more realistic version of awkward teenagehood. It's only after David's death that Keanu gets to show some depth, carrying the burden of knowledge of his friend's suicide and deciding whether he should tell anyone else – his school friends, David's parents. The audience are brought into Chris' struggle through Keanu's skilful acting. Overall, *Permanent Record* manages to orchestrate a

Keanu displayed his excellent acting skills in Permanent Record.

clever discussion of some difficult issues, while remaining well grounded in drama and character.

'The high school years are a difficult time in people's lives,' said Mancuso Jr of the inspiration behind *Permanent Record*. 'Today there is pressure on young people not to be left behind. You need good grades so you can get into the right school and later get a job that pays you what you need to make a decent living. That's a lot of responsibility for eighteen-year-olds to carry. Some of the pressure comes from having to make important choices before you know what it is you're deciding on. I wanted to make a movie that thoughtfully deals with these concerns.'

Mancuso Jr recruited Marisa Silver to bring his concept to the screen. Her first feature film as writer-director had been *Old Enough*, which had been honoured at the United States Film Festival and the Houston Film Festival. Silver was an Emmy-nominated documentary film-maker who was in the process of making the switch to dramatic features.

The biggest hurdle Silver faced was casting the film. Filling the ensemble roles with well-known names was not an option – and not only for budgetary reasons. 'I was looking for young people who had an idiosyncratic quality about them,' felt Silver. 'We didn't want characters you could easily categorise. It was important to find actors who you wouldn't be able to figure out the first time you saw them on the screen because the story is about how their personalities change as a result of what happens.'

Having cast Alan Boyce in the short-lived role of David Sinclair, Silver turned her attention to filling the main part, best friend Chris Townsend. Keanu had a definite take on the character. 'Chris is easy-going, but has a *joie de vivre* that makes him reckless at times,' said Keanu. 'He isn't a good student. Music and playing in the band are what's important to him. His friend, David, is his inspiration. When David dies, that loss brings Chris the most pain he has ever felt. His world is torn apart, but David's death teaches Chris a lesson about life.'

For Mancuso Jr there was much in Keanu that recommended his casting. 'We were looking for an actor to portray someone who is constantly on the edge; someone who is always pushing the walls out, seeing how far he can go; someone with real highs and lows. Keanu was able to convey that.'

Permanent Record was filmed in Portland and on the coast of Oregon. 'The story could happen anywhere at anytime to anyone. We selected the Northwest because it's such a beautiful environment. We didn't want the surroundings to be oppressive. The film is ultimately about life and we wanted the environment to be one of regeneration – the kind of environment found in the Northwest.'

Keanu plays Chris Townsend, a young musician who has to cope with the suicide of his best friend.

Keanu's character Chris is torn apart when his best friend David (Alan Boyce) dies.

Important to the effect of the film and central to its story is music. 'Concerns of young people today are reflected in the music,' said Becky Mancuso, the music supervisor for *Permanent Record*. Joe Strummer, of the Clash, composed the film's score and wrote several original songs to give the film a sense of the angst of youth. Rock icon Lou Reed makes a cameo appearance as a famous rock star encountered by David and Chris when they illicitly gain entrance to a studio session at the beginning of the film.

With Paramount Studios behind the film and a budget of $8 million, *Permanent Record* proved to be an incident-free shoot for Keanu, a film he enjoyed doing, but not one that he considered significant in his career, depite positive press notices.

The powerful message of *Permanent Record* was broadly welcomed by the critics. For *Variety*, 'Keanu Reeves' performance opens up nicely as the drama progresses.' For the *Los Angeles Times*, Keanu showed a 'relaxed vitality and unwavering honesty' in the film. The critic on the *Boston Globe* noted that Keanu was 'a young actor of depth and remarkably sure instincts'.

He may have had the right instincts to strike a chord with people who saw *Permanent Record*, but Keanu's instincts sometimes deserted him when it came to selecting roles. That appeared to be the case when he agreed to take a part in *The Night Before*.

This would-be comedy was narrated in flashback, às Keanu's character awoke in the path of an oncoming truck and then proceeded to piece together what had

Teen King: Permanent Record *allowed Keanu to portray a character with real depth.*

happened to him the previous evening. The standard prom-date-goes-wrong teen movie then unfolds, as Keanu dates Lori Loughlin (whom he'd featured beside in *The Brotherhood of Justice*). Ending up in a down-market club, the duo enjoy a series of unfunny misadventures as they struggle to get to their prom.

Director Thom Eberhart shepherded this all-too-familiar tale through to its conclusion, failing to capitalise on Keanu's clear abilities, as displayed in both *River's Edge* and *Permanent Record*. Perhaps an upbeat comedy was not what Keanu was in tune with at that time, so his by-the-numbers performance is less of a disappointment than it might have been. In any event, *The Night Before* was to enjoy a very limited release, a fact which suited Keanu Reeves down to the ground. 'It's a coming-of-age movie,' said Keanu. 'You know, guy wants girl, guy gets girl. I was in every scene – a hungover dweeb. . .'

Becoming somewhat more choosy about his roles after *The Night Before*, Keanu Reeves turned down the leading role in the special effects horror sequel to David Cronenberg's remake of *The Fly*, continuing instead to plough a furrow in the world of offbeat teen movies. *The Prince of Pennsylvania* was just the right kind of film to catch Keanu's eye.

A quirky character comedy revolving around a madcap kidnapping scheme, Keanu got to take his dazed teen persona to its extreme. He plays Rupert Marshetta, a member of a perfect middle-class family headed by Fred Ward as his father Gary and Bonnie Bedelia as Pam, his mother. Rupert is not willing to be part of the perfect American dream; with his shock haircut (short on one side, long on the other) and his laid-back attitude to matters of education and vocation, he's not about to follow in his father's hard-working footsteps to the local coal-mines.

He instead pursues Carla (Amy Madigan), an older ex-hippie whom Rupert sees as feminine sexuality incarnate, despite the fact that she's half-heartedly involved with the local policeman. As father Gary feels he is losing his grip on his family, when it comes to light that his wife has been having an affair with his best friend, he decides to send Rupert down the mines whether he likes it or not. The scene is set for a bizarre climax, as Rupert resolves that the only solution to everyone's problems is a complicated scheme to kidnap his father and have his mother sell the mine to raise a ransom.

The Prince of Pennsylvania was the brainchild of writer-director Ron Nyswaner, who had scripted such films as *Mrs Soffell* and *Smithereens*. The film was his directorial debut and he chose to set it in a milieu he knew – his home town in the coal-mining suburbs of Pennsylvania. During production he would take his cast and crew on extensive tours of the area to give them a feeling for a working-class world where town life revolves around the mines. 'The people in the area loved the fact that we were making a movie there,' recalled Nyswaner. 'In one town we wanted to get some night exteriors, and they shut down the whole town for us. Then we needed a high angle shot and the local fire department allowed us to use their 100-foot ladder for the effect.'

In one scene in the film where Keanu as Rupert joins a raid by a local motorcycle gang on a high school dance, he was the only professional actor. The rest of the extras in the scene consisted of locals rounded up by Nyswaner's crew. 'That was certainly frightening for a first time director,' he admitted. 'One hundred and fifty extras, including high school students and real bikers with their own motorcycles. Actually, the bikers were wonderful to work with. One night they did get a little too drunk and we had to cancel their scenes, but for the most part they were co-operative and charming. I went to high school with some of them.'

In the end, *The Prince of Pennsylvania* failed to make the grade, being an entertaining rather than profound look at middle-class life in late-'80s America. Having been acclaimed in *River's Edge*, Keanu now found himself the object of several critics' derision for his role in *The Prince of Pennsylvania*.

David Edelstein in the *Village Voice* reserved most of his criticism for Nyswaner as director, feeling he took too much note of Nyswaner the writer. 'He can't make the kidnap plot plausible (it really is a pathetically dumb idea, with no chance of working), and he can't get the tone right in the second half. He can make everyday absurdities resonate like crazy . . . Keanu has some self-conscious charm, but his emotions are generalised. He doesn't risk anything, and his shambling sheep-dog blurriness keeps the film from having any sustained power.'

The film fared no better critically in the British press. David Robinson in *The Times* called the film 'well intentioned . . . transparently schematic, with the characters drawn in two dimensions', while Richard Mayne, in the *Sunday Telegraph*, felt the film 'creates a real sense of claustrophobic place and class, but the plot develops from a teenage fantasy, and never escapes it, despite a witty and literate script.'

Despite the critical mauling, Keanu was pleased with his work in *The Prince of Pennsylvania*, and didn't worry too much that it wasn't a hit at the box office. Like *River's Edge*, the film was to enjoy a successful afterlife on video. 'Thank heavens

Keanu teamed up again with Lori Loughlin for the comedy The Night Before.

Bad hair day: Keanu tries a new look as Rupert Marshetta in The Prince of Pennsylvania.

for home video,' said Keanu. 'It gives little pictures like that a second chance.' It also helped kick-start the actor's early career.

With *The Prince of Pennsylvania* under his belt, Keanu Reeves felt it was time to pack in playing teenagers. He had more than his fair share of teen roles, and now at almost 24 it was getting harder and harder to pass for seventeen, even with his baby-faced good looks. It had been some time since the self-declared Shakespeare buff had been able to tackle anything remotely literary on stage or on film, and he was feeling rather the worse for it. A chance to feature in the film *Dangerous Liaisons* seemed ideal, no matter how out of left field it may have seemed to cast teen idol Keanu Reeves in a costume drama. After all, felt the young actor, this was probably as close to playing Shakespeare on screen as he was likely to get, so he'd better take the opportunity while it was offered.

The film version of *Dangerous Liaisons* originated from the 1782 novel, *Les Liaisons Dangereuses*, by Choderlos de Laclos. This erotic and psychological masterpiece, written as a series of letters and now taught on university literature courses, had enjoyed a scandalous reputation and endured numerous bannings since its original publication.

British playwright Christopher Hampton was one who had found himself caught up in the book's spell. 'I loved the book and used to re-read it often. It's one of the most profound analyses ever made of love and sex – and the difference between them.'

His long-harboured ambition of turning the book into a stage play came in 1984, when he was commissioned by the Royal Shakespeare Company to write anything he chose. The play went on to win the 1986 Olivier Award, ran for over 800 performances in London, and has played around the world, including on Broadway and in Paris.

The possibility of a film version of the play had followed soon after its London première in 1986. Director Stephen Frears, who had developed his craft on British TV and with such low budget quirky films as *My Beautiful Laundrette* and *Prick Up Your Ears*, was soon involved. '*Dangerous Liaisons* has such a wonderful story,' said Frears. 'The setting may be just before the French Revolution, but it is very modern in its treatment of romance. People behaving badly is quite familiar.'

Hampton scripted the film, but rather than adapt his play, he returned to the original source material, the book itself. 'I really put the play away, started from the book again and tried to rethink it. The way you build a scene in the theatre is different, it takes more time to develop.'

Set among the French aristocracy just prior to the French Revolution, *Dangerous Liaisons* takes place in a time of legendary decadence. The wealthy characters in the tale are fully dedicated to the pursuit of their own pleasures – pleasures which are enhanced if they are gained at the misery of others not so fortunate. Prime among the schemers and manipulators of the tale are ex-lovers the Marquise de Merteuil and the Vicomte de Valmont. The story concerns a series of seductions and would-be seductions orchestrated by these two characters in a mad game of emotional and romantic one-upmanship.

Casting was as difficult for Frears as reinventing the tale for the cinema was for Hampton. Although Hampton redrafted the story from the book, much of the actual dialogue came from his play, so Frears determined to have actors with some theatrical training who could handle the theatrical nature of the dialogue. However, with thoughts of the box office never far from his mind, the director also knew he needed actors who would draw an audience into what could be potentially a rather difficult piece of work. 'To me, the access to the material is through the characters,' explained the director. 'The film is about people dealing with their feelings, or failing to deal with them, and American actors play feelings wonderfully, especially in close up.'

Glenn Close, stage trained and fresh from *Fatal Attraction*, was a natural choice at the time to play the scheming Merteuil. 'It's a part I always wanted to play,' she said. 'She's very modern – a highly intelligent woman born in the wrong century. She really has no outlets for her brilliance, except for manipulation.'

Pitched against her as the seducer Valmont was John Malkovich. 'Valmont is born with so many advantages,' Malkovich felt. 'He's intelligent, witty, clever, rich and attractive, yet he devotes himself to destruction. All this wit and drive and passion and talent and energy devoted to decadence could have only one result: revolution.'

Malkovich developed a protective attitude to his young co-star on the movie. Of Keanu he said: 'He's the archetypal troubled young American, like your younger brother or someone you should be helping out. He doesn't invite it, but if you're older you feel like you should protect him.'

When Merteuil's intended husband, Comte de Bastide, abandons her for the virginal Cecile de Volanges (Uma Thurman, then aged eighteen), she enlists the aid

Keanu gets physical with John Malkovich in the climax of Dangerous Liaisons.

of Valmont, by trying to persuade him to seduce Volanges and so upset Bastide. Valmont, however, is more interested in the challenge presented by the very married and very moral Madame de Tourvel (Michelle Pfeiffer). Caught up in all these shenanigans is young music teacher Chevalier Darceny (Keanu Reeves), who has taken a fancy to his latest pupil: Cecile de Volanges.

Pfeiffer was alone in the cast in having no stage experience as even the younger duo of Keanu and Thurman had practised their craft on stage to varying degrees. For Keanu, the part meant a very welcome trip to Paris in May 1988, where the film was shot on location in a series of eight magnificent chateaux on the outskirts of the city. To ensure the realism of the film a French Count was enlisted to instruct the cast and crew on the finer points of 18th-century etiquette, and the actors found themselves thrust into restricting corsets and high collared outfits, their heads topped with giant, flamboyant wigs.

Well versed in acting for the cameras, Keanu did have one major problem while shooting *Dangerous Liaisons* – crying on cue. Required to shed tears in an early scene of the film at the opera, the young actor found he couldn't make the tears come to order, despite increasingly frustrated exhortations from director Stephen Frears. 'Can't you think of your mother being dead or something?' was one charming technique Keanu claimed Frears suggested to him. After several hours he finally pulled off what seemed to be his most difficult acting challenge in his career so far – getting tears to flow.

His part in the film was a pivotal one for Keanu. Though reduced somewhat from the original script, where he was to have enjoyed an affair with Glenn Close,

Keanu was nonetheless fairly heavily featured in the film – he was, after Malkovich, the second male lead. He even enjoyed the opportunity to participate in a climactic fencing duel with Malkovich, a chance to apply the skills he'd learned for his stage role in *Romeo and Juliet* in 1985.

From his work with Stephen Frears, Keanu was to develop a liking for working with European directors, an ambition he would fulfil in films with Bernardo Bertolucci, Kenneth Branagh and Jan De Bont. 'There's more poetry in [Frears's] work,' he said. 'I guess that there's – not a romantic – but a more obvious sensibility to sight, sound, smell, taste, touch and how profound all of those senses are. And in the relationship between speaking and moving, [Frears] seems to be closer to that part of movie-making.'

The film was shot in a mere ten weeks – not for budgetary reasons, as Frears had $14 million to play with, five times his previous highest budget – but because a rival production was breathing down their necks. Director Milos Forman had discussed shooting a version of the *Dangerous Liaisons* tale with Christopher Hampton, as Frears's version was getting off the ground. Deciding not to tackle the play, but to produce a version of the public domain book, Forman launched his production, entitled *Valmont*. In fact, the book had also been filmed once before, in 1960 by French film-maker Roger Vadim.

The *Dangerous Liaisons* team need not have worried. Forman's cast of Colin Firth and Meg Tilly hardly compared with the dynamic teaming of Glenn Close and John Malkovich. *Dangerous Liaisons* easily beat *Valmont* into the cinemas, with a Christmas 1988 release also handily putting the film into eligibility for Oscar nominations. There were seven nominations, with three being awarded – for Art Direction, Screenplay and, of course, Costumes. Although nominated for their acting, neither Close nor Malkovich was successful.

Reviews of *Dangerous Liaisons* were mixed. *Newsweek* called the film 'nasty decadent fun', and *People* said that it '. . . makes characters of 200 years ago seem as near as next door . . . seductive, scary, savagely witty'.

For many reviewers, however, the casting of *Dangerous Liaisons* was both inspired and problematic – inspired in the case of Glenn Close and Michelle Pfeiffer, and problematic when it came to John Malkovich and Keanu Reeves. *Variety* said 'Glenn Close is admirably cast as the proud, malevolent Merteuil, while the real problem is Malkovich's Valmont. The sly actor conveys the character's snaky, premeditated Don Juanism, but he lacks the devilish charm and seductiveness one senses Valmont would need to carry off all his conquests.'

For some, Keanu's presence in the film presented a credibility threshold which the film was never able to cross. According to the *New York Post*, for example, Keanu was 'howlingly out of place' in period costume in *Dangerous Liaisons*. Known for his edgy teen roles, the audience didn't take to him as an upright French piano teacher, and Keanu himself sometimes seemed uncomfortable in the part. As soon as they had come to terms with Glenn Close's wicked witch turn and Malkovich's fey performance, then in bounced Keanu, clearly overshadowed by the other actors.

Many agreed that Keanu did come into his own, however, in the physical clash he has with Malkovich at the film's climax. In the sword fight and the sequences after, when he hears Malkovich's confession and becomes his *post mortem* messenger, Keanu justifies his presence in the film. It's a shame that the editing of the script before shooting resulted in Keanu's Chevalier Darceny suggested affair with Close's Marquise becoming all but lost, as it would have ensured an added frisson to his part.

Despite the attacks on Keanu for having the audacity to tackle a part in a flowery, literary costume drama, *Dangerous Liaisons* was to prove an important turning point for the young actor. With *Dangerous Liaisons* Keanu had finally shaken off the teen parts that had dogged his career for years, and had moved on to playing young adults. Also, without this first dipping of his toe into the waters of cinematic costume drama, it is unlikely that he would have eventually fulfilled his dream of playing Shakespeare on screen in Kenneth Branagh's *Much Ado About Nothing*, four years later.

As his acting career had taken off and Keanu Reeves began to reap the financial benefits, he developed a love of speed, expressed through his ownership and reckless riding of a variety of high powered motorcycles.

Having dumped his original cheap and cheerful bike purchased when he first arrived in LA, Keanu now owned a Moto Guzzi and enjoyed the use of a hired Harley. Later he'd own a 1972 Combat Norton and a 1974 850 Norton Commando. He enjoyed racing through the streets of Los Angeles at night, often without a helmet and without his lights on. He explained away this recklessness as his way of letting off steam, of escaping the pressures he sometimes felt under as difficult movie choices lay before him. Others saw his risk-taking from a different point of view – he was a young man testing his own mortality. His quest for speed was not without its cost, as Keanu took frequent tumbles from his bikes, some of them very serious.

Between auditioning in New York for the role of Chevalier Darceny in *Dangerous Liaisons* and eventually winning the part, Keanu had a close brush with death when he was involved in a serious motorcycle crash in Topanga Canyon, outside Los Angeles. So seriously was the young actor injured in this crash that his ruptured spleen was removed, leaving the now famous prominent scar which runs from his lower chest all the way down to his navel – presenting a distinct problem for film make-up artists in those films which required Keanu to remove his top.

Recovering in hospital and scared by the accident, Keanu was still not persuaded to give up his passion for bikes. He was to suffer further, more minor, smashes in coming years, but still insisted on riding the bikes. 'I have a scar on my knee, a very small one. I was on my motorcycle, and I got hit by a car on the corner of Hollywood and Normandie. The car was making a left, and I jumped from the motorcycle, just before the guy hit me. I did a somersault in the air and landed on the sidewalk on my back,' recalled Keanu of one of his motorcycle smashes.

'The man, who eventually drove me to hospital, said to me: "You are in the air, and I think to myself, that boy – he is dead. Then you jumped up. I could not believe it." As I was waiting for the ambulance, these two boys, about eight or nine, came by and they had big, wide eyes. I looked up at them and said, "I flew, didn't I?" They went, "You were in the air, bro. . ." I was totally laughing. I totalled my bike.'

When not falling off his bike, or wrapping his mouth around literary language in costume dramas, Keanu had plenty of other opportunities to indulge his new-found wealth on leisure activities. 'I dig going out,' he told *Interview* magazine in 1990. 'I have fun. I don't get many invitations and stuff – it's just kind of whatever happens. Once in a while I'll ask my friends, "What're you doing? Where are you going? What's going on?" I'll go see art, I'll do whatever – buy a drink, dance, play. All that shit. Sometimes I go to clubs. I dig the blues, man. The blues have always had some of the best times, best feelings I've ever had. The last person I saw was Buddy Guy, but it was in a bad space, just bummed me out.'

Living and working in Los Angeles, Keanu Reeves had plenty of opportunities to form relationships, but even at almost 24 years of age he was still finding it difficult. He had trouble maintaining relationships with those women whom he did hook up with, a seeming hangover from his own insecurity as a child, the departure of his father and the series of pseudo-fathers he'd had in his life. 'On the weekends I've been kinda cruising the boulevards. LA is so trippy. On those weekend nights the prostitutes are out, and the kids from school, and people cruising, and in the clubs all that stuff is going on.'

However, for Keanu 'all that stuff' – relationships, romance, love and sex – seemed less important than the solitude he gained riding around on his motorcycle at speeds beyond those that were good for him. 'I ride my bike sometimes. I'll just go out, around one, midnight, and I'll ride until four. Goin' through the city to see who's doin' what, where, y'know. Going downtown, riding around and just looking around. Yeah, great. . .'

CHAPTER FOUR

Keanu's Excellent Adventure

O UT OF HIS PERIOD COSTUME and having survived his brush with death in his motorcycle accident, Keanu Reeves had to decide where his career was to go as a new decade dawned. The last thing he thought would happen was that a low budget time travel comedy he'd made two years previously – *Bill and Ted's Excellent Adventure* – would finally be released and give him a higher public profile than ever before.

For now, however, Keanu gave great thought to how he could escape his previous 'troubled teen' typecasting. He was in his 25th year, even if he was still able to look about sixteen for each of his roles in films like *Permanent Record* and *The Night Before.*

'If all you do is symbolise the youth of your time,' said Keanu thoughtfully, 'then you're going to burn out as soon as they grow up and there's a new youth in search of a new symbol. I won't mention any names, but that has happened to a lot of people.'

The risk was that if he did another film like *Dangerous Liaisons*, something far removed from what his teen audience expected, then the actor's growing number of fans would not be willing to see it. There was some subtle repositioning required – and Keanu was smart enough to know that he had to change his image and widen his roles slowly rather than with one, big dramatic film. In the meantime the comedy-drama *Parenthood*, directed by Ron Howard, kept him occupied.

Howard had been a one-time child star on American TV, featuring in *The Andy Griffith Show* and as Richie Cunningham in '70s sitcom *Happy Days*, best friend of Henry Winkler's Fonz. He started his movie directing career with well-known low budget king Roger Corman, alongside Francis Ford Coppola and Martin Scorsese, before directing the old-age-and-aliens fantasy *Cocoon* in 1985. Howard's idea for *Parenthood* had developed from the time when he himself became a parent for the first time, nine years before he had the chance to actually make the film.

For *Parenthood*, Keanu Reeves was part of a huge ensemble cast, including Steve Martin, Dianne Wiest, Mary Steenburgen, Jason Robards and Tom Hulce. However, he was again playing the troubled teen, as Tod, the boyfriend of Martha Plimpton's sixteen-year-old Julie. Keanu topped a list of young actors with proven box office appeal that Howard had drawn up for the role.

A variety of mini-plots and soap opera-like relationship dramas unfold throughout *Parenthood*, laced with rich humour that draws out laughs of

Keanu with Martha Plimpton in Parenthood; *she was River Phoenix's girlfriend.*

recognition from most audiences. Steve Martin plays Gil, who is trying hard to make sure he's a better father to his three kids than his father (Jason Robards) was for him. Gil's sister Helen (played by Wiest) has her own problems with daughter Julie – who eventually becomes pregnant by Keanu's Tod – and her video-addicted son Garry (Leaf Phoenix). His brother Rick Moranis has an over-achieving only daughter who puts Martin's own kids into the shade. Into this mix comes long lost brother Larry (Tom Hulce), a gambling addict who can do no wrong in the eyes of clan patriarch Robards – until even he cannot turn a blind eye to his conman antics.

Terrence Rafferty, writing in the *New Yorker*, saw the film as 'ambitiously constructed. . .Howard has assembled a first-rate cast, including Keanu Reeves. They all work hard at giving life to the movie's schematic characters.' *Rolling Stone* noted: '*Parenthood* packs its observations with a sting.'

Variety called *Parenthood* 'an ambitious, keenly observed and often very funny look at one of life's most daunting passages. *Parenthood* 's masterstroke is that it covers the range of family experience, offering the points of view of everyone in an extended and wildly diverse middle-class family.'

From his work on *Parenthood*, Keanu Reeves developed a great and lasting friendship with River Phoenix. 'I met Keanu through my ex-girlfriend Martha [Plimpton] while they were doing *Parenthood* – they were sucking face regularly,' recalled River Phoenix. 'My brother Leaf was also in it, so Leaf and Martha were his buddies before I even became a friend of his. I liked the guy and I wanted to work with him. He's like my older brother, but shorter . . .'

Their friendship was to continue through *I Love You to Death* where they worked together briefly and into *My Own Private Idaho*, the film that began Phoenix's downward spiral into drug addiction and eventual premature death. Keanu was to remain a close friend of Phoenix right to the end, and the death of his young co-star was to have a profound effect on him, changing his attitude to drugs and giving him a keener sense of his own mortality, on and off-screen.

A scene-stealing bit part was next on Keanu Reeves's acting agenda in *I Love You to Death* (1990), a black-as-pitch farce based on a true story.

The film told the tale of womanising pizza restaurant owner, Joey Boca (Kevin Kline) whose disenchanted wife Rosalie (Tracey Ullman) determines to kill him, in cahoots with New-Age pizza restaurant worker Devo Nod (River Phoenix). However, Joey is made of strong stuff and survives a car bomb, an overdose of poison hidden in a huge pasta serving and a bullet in the head.

As Tod in Parenthood *Keanu was able to indulge his need for speed in the film's racing scenes.*

As the desperation of Ullman and Phoenix rises, they call in a pair of spaced-out hitmen, played by William Hurt and Keanu Reeves. Harlon and Marlon James turn out to be as incompetent at doing the deed as the rest of the family. *I Love You To Death* was based on real life events from the lives of Anthony and Frances Toto and Barry Giacobe, with the usual embellishments that any true-story-to-film conversion undergoes in Hollywood.

Producer Ron Moler got hold of the story in 1984, his curiosity captured by reports of five unsuccessful attempts on Anthony's life by his jealous wife who had been shocked to discover he'd had a string of affairs. Amazingly, the couple were reunited after his wife, Frances had served out her jail sentence. It was ideal

Happy families: Keanu as Marlon James, a dumb hitman hired to bump off Kevin Kline's Joey Boca in the black comedy I Love You To Death.

comedy feature film material, so Moler set about developing the script, with co-producer Patrick Wells and screenwriter John Kostmayer.

Tacoma in Washington was the location for the filming of *I Love You To Death*, which started on 10 April 1989. The interior shots which featured Hurt and Keanu were, however, filmed later in Hollywood at the Raleigh studios. Keanu had been selected by director Lawrence Kasdan, based on his performance in *River's Edge* and a recommendation from Ron Howard, director of *Parenthood*.

Meeting co-star William Hurt in rehearsals, Keanu was overwhelmed by the more experienced, somewhat serious actor. 'I was really awed at first – William Hurt! He's such an incredible actor . . . a real serious guy . . .' Keanu took advantage of the presence of both Hurt and Kline to ply the more seasoned actors with questions about their craft. Always wanting to learn more, Keanu would take any opportunity to discover how other actors approached their work.

For Keanu, freedom from strict direction resulted in him and Hurt collaborating on their wild portrayals. Said Keanu: 'Sometimes I don't mind being left alone [by the director]. It all depends on where I am personally and the feeling of the piece. On *I Love You To Death*, Lawrence Kasdan let me go, so I just went flying. It's not necessarily a bad thing. My guy was just harmless. Larry Kasdan wanted the guy to be beat up by the world, just kind of in a daze. Harmless and drugged – so they hired me!'

Keanu thoroughly enjoyed his bit-part slumming in *I Love You To Death*. He and William Hurt proved to be the star turns of the film, as their high-as-kites characters struggle to conclude their contract, shepherded by River Phoenix. With conversations riddled with pregnant pauses and unfinished sentences, as well as a distracted William Hurt brushing away seemingly invisible flies, Marlon and Harlon almost stole the film from under the nose of River Phoenix.

When it opened almost exactly a year after production, on 11 April 1990, a decidedly mixed response greeted *I Love You To Death*. It seemed to be too blackly comic, certainly for most mainstream American audiences. Many reviewers picked up on the hilarious cameo appearance by Hurt and Keanu, with *Rolling Stone* writer Peter Travers calling the duo 'one of the oddest screen couplings of recent years. William Hurt and Keanu Reeves have a ball as two addled druggies brought in to finish Joey off with a bullet in the chest.'

The Times spotlighted the pair's antics: 'William Hurt and Keanu Reeves ham it up as excessively as Kline's manic macho Italian', while the *Guardian* felt the pair were 'embarrassingly inept as two hired dumb-as-oxen killers'.

After making *River's Edge*, Keanu Reeves had committed to what he regarded as a silly film which seemed likely to be little more than a fun job. He had completed the shooting of *Bill and Ted's Excellent Adventure* in May 1987, between making *The Night Before* and *Permanent Record*, but the film was to languish on the distributor's shelf for over two years, during which time the young man quietly forgot about it. In 1989, though, Theodore Logan III made something of a dramatic re-entry into the life and career of Keanu Reeves.

Writers Chris Matheson and Ed Solomon had concocted a fairly basic time travel story which had two dumb-but-lovable high-schoolers journeying through the ages in order to complete their history education. The characters had grown out of improvisations and letters between Matheson and Solomon, and were to develop into a feature length script. Matheson – son of Richard Matheson, a writer on Rod Serling's classic *Twilight Zone* TV series – said the 'valley speak' adopted by Bill and Ted grew out of the characters. 'Our original suggestion was "fifteen-year-old boys talk about world affairs". We had them talking about world trouble spots and trade problems, but their only impression of anything going on in the world was that it was "bogus"! Ed and I went out after the [improv] show that night and played those guys for about three hours. We fleshed them out, and many things fell into place that are still there.'

The team spent about two years working on the script. 'Our initial take was wild, loose and unstructured – which gave it a crazy irreverence – but it became much more organised. The device of time travel also changed. Originally we had Rufus [Bill and Ted's mentor from the future, played by George Carlin] driving them around through history in a '69 chevy van, but there was a feeling that it was too much like *Back to the Future*. When [director] Steve Herek came on board, he suggested the phone booth and it works pretty well.' Herek and the writers seemed unaware that British TV had featured a time-travelling character who'd used a phone booth as his mode of transport since 1963 in the long-running TV series *Doctor Who*.

'William Hurt's a real serious guy,' said Keanu of working with his I Love You To Death *co-star.*

Film producer Scott Kroopf loved the script as soon as he read it and leapt on the project with some enthusiasm. 'We immediately optioned it and within 24 hours got a call from Warner Brothers.' That initial excitement soon petered out as years were to go by before the project moved beyond this initial stage of interest. 'We went into business with them, through a development project that lasted four years, at the end of which they said they didn't want to do it! So we took it to the DeLaurentiis Entertainment Group.' Although the film went into production under the DeLaurentiis banner, that was not to be the end of the troubles for *Bill and Ted's Excellent Adventure*.

At the time *Bill and Ted's Excellent Adventure* finally got the go-ahead, time travel movies were undergoing something of a revival, with Terry Gilliam's *Time Bandits*, Francis Ford Coppola's *Peggy Sue Got Married* and *My Science Project* all having been recently released. Matheson, though, saw his film as more than a mere gimmicky time travel flick. 'This is a character piece,' he said. 'It's establishing these two goofy guys and sending them back in time. I hope that it's funnier than the others – I didn't like any of them, except *Time Bandits*, it's the only one that had any originality.'

For Keanu Reeves, the character of Ted was clear. He'd played a serious version of the confused teen before in *River's Edge, The Night Before* and would do so afterwards in *Permanent Record*. In *Bill and Ted's Excellent Adventure* he saw an opportunity to try his hand at a more comic portrayal of the life of a modern teenager, to combine his previous acting roles with Matheson and Solomon's script to create a comically confused teen.

Cast as Bill was Alex Winter, an actor with ambitions that lay beyond the screen in writing and directing. Growing up in St Louis, Winter had appeared opposite horror film great Vincent Price in a production of *Oliver!* Work in commercials followed, as well as a tour of America in the 1977 revival of *The King and I*. Film work followed, alternating between the teen vampire flick *The Lost Boys* with Kiefer Sutherland, art movies like *Rosalie Goes Shopping* and box office flop *Haunted Summer*. Comedy attracted Winter, though, and he teamed up with Tom Stern for *The Idiot Box* on MTV. Later he'd write and co-direct *Hideous Mutant Freakz* (also known as *Freaked*), with a surprise appearance by Keanu Reeves.

Although it is hard now to imagine the characters of Bill and Ted being played by anyone but Alex Winter and Keanu Reeves, the casting process for the first film was a tortuous one. Keanu recalled an endless series of 'auditions, pretty intense ones. Gruelling. By the end of it, though, there were, like, ten guys. We [he and Winter] would alternate with each other and go into this room and read scenes.'

Scott Kroopf and Stephen Herek knew the importance of finding the right team to play their central characters, as the success of the film depended heavily on the charisma and relationship between the two actors and the characters. 'The first day I went in,' recalled Keanu, '[Alex] and I did our thing, then we were paired off with, like, 85 different guys – but we ended up together in the room at the end of the day, and we thought, "All right!"' There was some confusion at the beginning, though. 'I thought I was Bill,' claimed Keanu. 'And I thought I was Ted,' admitted Winter.

Shooting for *Bill and Ted's Excellent Adventure* took place in March, April and May 1987 at the recently closed Phoenix High School in Los Angeles. For Stephen Herek *Bill and Ted's Excellent Adventure* was only his second film, following his low budget *Gremlins*-inspired homage, *Critters*. Time travel and special effects weren't the attraction for Herek, who like Matheson, felt that the film's strengths lay in the characters. 'It's the relationship between Bill and Ted,' he claimed. 'That's what I really got caught up in, how symbiotic they were. They're like right and left – we can't have one without the other. It's a nice friendship.'

Keanu Reeves was too busy thoroughly enjoying the work at hand to be aware of the effect the film would have on his career two years into the future. 'This has really been a great deal of fun,' said Keanu of the movie, before talking about the scene he'd just been shooting. 'Ted really likes this. This final exam scene is his fantasy, with all of these cool, special lights – it's the culmination of all of his and Bill's efforts.' Two weeks of shooting also took place on location in Italy for the historical scenes featuring castles and coliseums, only the second time Keanu had travelled to Europe to shoot a film.

'All of the time travel is a sideline to the people in the film,' claimed Keanu, agreeing with director Herek and screenwriter Matheson in their analysis. 'It's not, here's a special effect, it's not ILM [Industrial Light and Magic, George Lucas's whizz-bang special effects factory]. These are earthy, homey special effects, which I'm looking forward to seeing.'

The fun of making *Bill and Ted's Excellent Adventure* appears to have been infectious, one of the reasons Herek thinks the film was ultimately successful despite all the obstacles put in its way. Incredibly, the director is quite cheerful about the fact that clearly in the background of some scenes, extras and other members of the cast can be seen laughing and grinning at the action the film's two dumb heroes are involved in. 'If you are having a good time, it comes across on screen. That's basically what I'm in this business for – everyone on set entering the spirit of fun, adventure and transmitting that to the audience.'

Keanu admitted that this kind of film was right up his street. As a big science fiction and comic-book fan, Keanu felt right at home in the middle of this adventure. 'I'm having the best time. I'm playing a guy who's so insouciant, a naive child of the woods, that it's fun and cleansing. And then to meet all these cool people!' Moreover, Keanu found his co-star Alex Winter to be a perfect partner. 'We work with each other all day,' Keanu had said during filming, 'and occasionally go out with the crew, but we basically only have each other to hang out with, and not go stir-crazy at night. It's very fortunate that we like each other – if we didn't, filming would be hell. Spending time together has certainly helped the work.'

In a burst of frankness, Keanu was honest enough during his work as Ted to realise that he was still on an uphill struggle when it came to acting. His teen roles had been very much like playing himself. Now he was having to be aware of the rhythms of comedy, and had to concentrate much more on maintaining a consistent character. Aware of his own limits, self-analysis and self-criticism was something that Keanu would return to again and again throughout his career, not needing critics to point out his technical shortcomings.

'Ted is hard when I don't have the energy,' admitted Keanu. 'I sometimes find myself commenting, in my performance, on Ted. There are certain things that Ted would do that almost become self-conscious. I don't know if that translates well, but that bothers me.

'Being consistent can be difficult,' continued Keanu, in his self-analytical mode. 'Getting the energy to bring out Ted has been the challenge – keeping up the energy, honesty and that whole look – it's hard to be a child of the woods in these times!'

After completion of the film, DeLaurentiis Entertainment Group went bankrupt, leaving the film stuck in limbo. 'We were desperate that the movie not just go to video immediately,' recalled producer Scott Kroopf of the options available. 'We got together with Nelson Entertainment; they made a low-ball offer on it and got it. At this point the movie had never been previewed, but it turned out to be very successful.'

Shelved upon completion in 1987, *Bill and Ted's Excellent Adventure* wasn't to reach American cinemas until February 1989. In the meantime, Keanu Reeves had become somewhat better known. The release period of the film was very important to its slow-build success and good word-of-mouth vibes. 'We came out on President's Day, which was terrific for us,' said producer Scott Kroopf. 'I don't know if we could have competed in the summer.'

On its delayed cinema release, *Bill and Ted's Excellent Adventure* drew the expected teenage crowd, since that was the primary target audience, but didn't do great business. It was only upon video release that the quirky little film gained a widespread appreciative mainstream audience, who clicked in to thinking of the two leading characters as a kind of modern Laurel and Hardy adrift in a hostile universe.

Criticisms were made that the film somehow glorified stupidness – and this was long before the mid-'90s glut of dumb movies like *Dumb and Dumber*, *Forrest Gump*, *Kingpin* and *The Stupids*. 'I would like to go on record as saying that is the lamest argument I've ever heard,' said Winter of the accusation. 'It's such a stupid argument. Comedy, playing with idiots, is as old as drama itself, and isn't saying

Classic clowns: Alex Winter and Keanu give life to the not-so-smart teens Bill and Ted.

everybody should be an idiot and not read – it's just a way of making people laugh. It's valid. That's like saying Charlie Chaplin was instigating idiocy and walking funny.'

For Keanu the role brought him more name recognition than he'd had in his previous films. He claimed to like it best when 'moms and dads with their kids walk up. "Wow, thank you for that movie. My kid loves it." The kids are all staring wide-eyed. . .They say real nice things about it.'

Such was the unexpected success of the film that it was given a high profile release in the UK, opening on Easter weekend 1990. For Hugo Davenport in the *Daily Telegraph*, *Bill and Ted* 'works because of its zippy pace, dippy valley-speak dialogue and likeable performances'. For *Empire* magazine, *Bill and Ted's Excellent Adventure* had a 'bizarre and endearing flavour', sporting 'outrageously witty Californian dialogue' and delivering 'a fast-paced comedy'. They had high praise for Keanu and Winter, finding them 'endearing in their vacuousness and party-hearty benevolence'.

Although not a mega-blockbuster upon its release in cinemas, *Bill and Ted's Excellent Adventure* was a financial success story. The film had cost $10 million to make, and when eventually released in 1989 it went on to make $45 million in cinemas in the United States alone. Further profits were generated through foreign release and home video.

Although its success was late in coming, taking the role in *Bill and Ted's Excellent Adventure* had a remarkable effect on Keanu Reeves's nascent career. He was catapulted from being a journeyman teen actor who had had a few decent roles (*River's Edge* prime among them) to being perceived as a comic genius who had captured a precise caricature of American youth at a specific time.

In all, Keanu was positive about this unexpected turn of events. After all, he'd put the film to the back of his mind in 1987, not expecting it to actually see the light of day. 'I like Ted,' he admitted. 'There is such joy to his outlook. He is a very sincere young man. He's a good guy, and he just wants to laugh and play rock 'n' roll, y'know. It's not that complicated.'

When the film became popular, Keanu discovered an unexpected downside to being seen as Ted. 'I'm always getting asked to be like Ted. In the streets most kids just wave at me or ask for an autograph, some try to get me to act like Ted, but I just say no. Then their faces fall and I feel so bummed, you know.'

However, the young actor was to find aspects of Ted useful in dealing with press interviews. For several years into the mid-'90s, Keanu would adopt a Ted-like persona when talking to journalists. 'Ted hung a label on me,' admitted Keanu, 'and I hung it on myself, to a certain extent.' It became a defence mechanism, a way of deflecting persistent questions away from his private life or his approach to acting.

As the years passed, however, it became only too clear that Keanu Reeves was simply not as daft as he liked to appear in public. 'No,' he said, 'I've never played stupid to keep someone distant. I don't play stupid. Either it's been a failure on my part to articulate, or my naiveté, or ingenuousness. . .you know, I find myself more able to give an explanation of a project five years later, rather than in the middle of it. It's so past-tense. I can tell you how I feel, but its context is harder to explain. Sometimes when I'm interviewed I'm not ready to do that, so I say "excellent". And you know what, man? It's okay!'

One thing he was sure about in his own mind was the reason for the success of the characters of Bill and Ted. 'I think Bill and Ted appeal on a lot of different

Alex Winter and Keanu as the dumb-but-lovable high-schoolers.

levels, at least to me. The child in me can dig watching them, but I also find a lot of the stuff they do very clever, and I just dig the "be excellent to each other" idea, you know. That's beautiful.'

One of his inspirations for his characterisation were some real-life friends. 'You know how [Bill and Ted] have their own language and say things like "bodacious" and "bogus", well, for a lot of my friends I know that sort of thing is true. These two guys I know can rap to each other and I don't even understand what they're saying.'

The language of the film struck a chord, and magazines at the time would print glossaries of Bill and Ted Speak to ease understanding of the film. Such was the success of the concept that a short-lived, animated, Saturday morning cartoon spin-off followed, with early episodes voiced by Keanu and Winter. There was also an attempt to turn the film into a live action sitcom, with less charismatic actors playing the Bill and Ted roles. Merchandising around the characters, from toys and games to breakfast cereals, also took off for a short while. However, Keanu did have one final thought about playing Ted and the success and recognition it had brought him in a relatively short period. 'When my life is over, I'll be remembered for playing Ted,' he lamented.

Escaping the spectre of Ted, Keanu got to turn his attention to something more theatrical, albeit a play staged on television. He won a major role in *Life Under Water*, an American Playhouse production of a play by Richard Greenberg. 'A sort of Holden Caulfield of the '80s,' is how Lindsay Law, executive director of American Playhouse, was to describe Keanu's character in this dramatic piece.

Following the intrigues of five bored but wealthy people holidaying in the Hamptons, *Life Under Water* was a chamber piece which gave Keanu and his co-star Sarah Jessica Parker plenty of opportunities to indulge themselves with their theatrical monologues and heavy, melancholy teeth gnashings. It was criticised, however, for being a play which did not really translate well into television.

Keanu was not clear why he'd taken the part, but inevitably the desire to do something as far removed from Ted as possible was part of his motivation, alongside his interest in doing a theatrical piece of work. Perhaps thankfully for its detractors, *Life Under Water* proved to be almost as ephemeral as a stage performance, as the show vanished without trace after broadcast.

Genuine theatrical experience awaited Keanu with a role in *The Tempest* as part of a summer workshop at Shakespeare and Company in Lennox, Massachusetts. As a result of previous classes and workshops he'd attended the year before, Keanu had been invited back to pay Trinculo, with Andre Gregory as Prospero. It was a brief, little noted run, but for Keanu it was his second significant attempt at playing Shakespeare on stage and laid some of the ground work for his later role as Hamlet. Although hard on the production as a whole, especially Gregory's interpretation of Prospero, the *Boston Globe* noted wryly that the audience greeted Keanu's appearances 'with something like eruptive joy'.

After *Life Under Water*, more unusual TV followed, with a guest appearance on *The Tracey Ullman Show*. Having impressed himself on Ullman during the shooting of *I Love You To Death*, the actress had offered Keanu a slot on her American TV variety and comedy show, which had been the launching pad for *The Simpsons* hit TV cartoon series.

Broadcast on 17 December 1989 as part of Ullman's Christmas show, *Two Lost Souls* was a comic skit which opened with Keanu waking, happy, to find himself in bed with Ullman. Playing teenager Jesse Walker, Keanu hops to his computer, about to compose a love letter to the woman in his bed. Ullman awakes, recovering from a New Year's Eve-induced hangover, only to realise with horror that she's not only slept with – but also married – the teenage son of her best friend. Ullman plays Barbara, the 35-year-old landscape artist who designed Jesse's parents' garden. Keanu plays a love-smitten teen well, making reference to film-maker Francois Truffaut, as well as to Dickens. Listed in the credits as a 'Special Appearance by Keanu Reeves', the lightly comic sketch was written by *The Tracey Ullman Show* producer Dinah Kirgo. What's more, Ullman got to smooch with Keanu, making her an instant enemy of teenage girls across America.

Like *Bill and Ted's Excellent Adventure*, the genesis and production of *Aunt Julia and the Scriptwriter* (titled *Tune in Tomorrow* in the United States) was tortuous and long drawn out. Interest in a film version of award-winning, Peruvian author Mario Vargas Llosa's 1977 comic magical realist novel had originally been shown in 1983 by producers Mark Tarlov and John Fiedler.

Enthusiastic about the possibility of a film version of the tale, they brought the project to Columbia Studios, then being run by British producer David Puttnam in a short-lived tenure. He brought screenwriter William Boyd and director Jon Amiel (who at that point was best known for his BBC TV version of Dennis Potter's *The*

Singing Detective) on board to work on the project. Unfortunately, Puttnam and the studio did not see eye-to-eye on a variety of matters and he had soon departed for fresh pastures, leaving the new regime to cancel the production of the movie version of *Aunt Julia and the Scriptwriter*.

Screenwriter William Boyd was faithful to the spirit of the book in his adaption of it for the screen, but he did alter characters, the plot and locations. It was a relief, therefore, when the production team behind the film received approval from the book's author for Boyd's screenplay. Now all that was required was for Amiel, Puttnam and Boyd to find a studio willing to back the film. A flirtation with MGM/UA didn't work out and the film finally found a home with independent production outfit Cinecom, but at a dramatically reduced budget of only $8 million – very low for what promised to be a costume-heavy period piece.

The story of *Aunt Julia and the Scriptwriter* opens in New Orleans in 1951 and is centred around Pedro (Peter Falk), a writer who steals from the lives

Real life fiction: Barbara Hershey, Peter Falk and Keanu in Aunt Julia and the Scriptwriter.

and speeches of people in real-life around him for the plots of the radio soap operas he creates. Enter 21-year-old Martin Loader (Keanu), a young man in a hurry who is in love with his 35-year-old aunt Julia (Barbara Hershey). In an attempt to play cupid, Pedro plagiarises their story, putting it out on the airwaves with few alterations to hide their identities. The story hops back and forth between Pedro's soap opera and the characters in it, creating a story-within-a-story. There is a large, oddball family played by John Larroquette, Buck Henry, Peter Gallagher and others, all concerned with the marriage of Elizabeth McGovern.

The key role in the film was that of Keanu's Martin Loader, the young seducer who proves to be a valuable source of romantic plot-lines for Pedro. 'There were a few young actors considered,' explained producer John Fiedler of filling the role, 'but we were pretty quick to go with Keanu Reeves. We just always saw him in the part.' Fiedler and Amiel had seen Keanu in *River's Edge*, like many other directors who had recently cast the actor in their films.

Barbara Hershey as Aunt Julia and Keanu as her young seducer, Martin Loader.

Said Amiel: 'I just loved the idea of casting Keanu Reeves, because when I met him, I saw the chance of having him play something I'd never even seen him come close to before. Most of the kids he plays are very freaky, eccentric and wild kids. I wanted him to play a young, Jimmy Stewart character – gawky, sincere, charming, bright – and adorable, for all those reasons.

'Barbara, Peter and Keanu made perfect sense to me. There soon came a point where, for me, they were their parts – the only ones who could possibly play them. That's when I knew the chemistry was right.'

Amiel's trust in his judgement was momentarily shaken when Keanu turned up to audition sporting his bizarre half-shaved hairstyle from *I Love You to Death*. Reassured that his hair would recover its normality before shooting, the trusting director was further perturbed when on the first day of the shoot Keanu turned up with perfect hair, but bandaged and limping after falling off his motorbike once more.

Despite his seemingly tardy approach to the film, Keanu had put in his usual diligent preparation, having studied the novel and spent time with a dialogue coach attempting to perfect a New Orleans accent. He'd also obtained an audio tape covering the history of New Orleans, which he would listen to at night in an attempt to absorb something of the ambience of the city.

The role of Martin Loader was a very different part for Keanu Reeves. It was his first romantic lead – a kind of dress rehearsal for the later *A Walk in the Clouds*. Romance proved not to be the young actor's strong point, though. He didn't meet co-star Barbara Hershey until the first rehearsals, and found playing the part of her

KEANU'S EXCELLENT ADVENTURE

confident young lover somewhat daunting. Dancing the jitterbug in rehearsals with Hershey brought the pair closer together physically and served to break the ice between the two stars.

Despite this initial awkwardness, Keanu was keen on the film and his role. 'What appealed to me was his spirit and passion,' said Keanu of his Martin Loader character. 'He's just about to break out of his repression.'

Although the film version was approved by the author, the marketing of the movie was somewhat fumbled. With Cinecom taken over halfway through production, the new studio bosses decided they didn't like the title, using test screening to show that audiences found it difficult to recall. For the American release the film was retitled *Tune in Tomorrow*, much to the chagrin of Jon Amiel, and advertised as a slapstick comedy likely to appeal to young males, instead of as a sophisticated, though funny, romance with definite female appeal.

This very different part for Keanu resulted in some of the best notices he'd received in his career so far. According to the *Los Angeles Times*, Keanu had 'an engaging presence' in the film, with 'a winning hang-dog lyricism', while *Entertainment Weekly* noted that 'with his short hair slicked back, Keanu has the outrageous glamour of a '30s matinee idol, and he gives his most winning performance yet . . .' However, where American audiences had taken the goofy star of *Bill and Ted's Excellent Adventure* to heart, European audiences remained sceptical of his true abilities, beyond the surface good looks and ability to incarnate clowns.

As the 1980s came to a close, Keanu Reeves was celebrating a personal milestone, as well as all the career milestones that 1989 had brought him. He turned 25 in September that year, and began for the first time to seriously think ahead. 'I was going along great coming up to being 25 and suddenly I passed it and started thinking, hey, I'm gonna die one day. I started looking at my mother in a different way. What's important? Who am I? Why am I here? It was weird. It was a radical experience. It was like I woke up one morning with a different mind-set. I wish I still had the old one, man . . .'

For Keanu age, fame and fortune also meant new responsibilities. His sister Kim, with whom the actor had remained very close since childhood, had developed cancer. Over the next six or seven years Keanu would spend a great deal of time looking after his sister, until the disease went into remission in 1995. The money he earned from the films was to prove very useful in this respect, and this new commitment to Kim also gave him further reason to continue with the career he had embarked upon.

'He helped me through,' Kim told *Vanity Fair*. 'When the pain got bad, he used to hold my hand and keep the bad man from making me dance. He was there all the time, even when he was away.'

Looking after Kim's needs became a motivating force for Keanu, and spending time with her during stays in Los Angeles hospitals became non-negotiable items on his busy schedule. He bought a stable of show horses for Kim, which she now manages, and he spent much time at her home, where many of the young film star's personal belongings were held in storage pending the day he ever bought a house of his own. 'My brother is a prince,' said Kim. 'He listens to every word, to every comma after every word, that you are saying.'

CHAPTER FIVE

Breaking Point

K EANU REEVES was – at age 25 – well established as one of Hollywood's up-and-coming young actors, with much potential yet to fulfil. Experimentation had been the hallmark of his last few roles, from the comedy of *I Love You to Death*, through to the romantic lead in *Aunt Julia and the Scriptwriter*. With the roles had come fame, with interviews appearing in teen magazine across the world at the launch of each new film.

Meanwhile his love life stayed out of the entertainment press. 'Love's an easy emotion, man,' he admitted. 'It's easy to love people.' Romance and long-term relationships continued to be things Keanu would deny himself, fearing the shadow of his father, and partly out of inexperience. 'But I kind of like to suffer,' he said. 'People don't respect artists who don't suffer.'

Suffering – in the physical rather than emotional sense – was just what awaited Keanu, when he signed up to star in the action movie *Point Break* (1991). Director Kathryn Bigelow had gathered something of a reputation as Hollywood's macho woman, with action-oriented films like vampire thriller *Near Dark* (1986) and cop thriller *Blue Steel* (1990), so it came as no surprise when she began work on something like *Point Break*.

The story of a maverick FBI agent who goes undercover among California's surfing community in order to solve a series of baffling bank raids, *Point Break* was ideal Bigelow material, allowing her to up the action movie stakes with spectacular surfing and sky-diving sequences as well as bank robberies, chases and gun play.

Point Break featured two leading characters – the improbably named Johnny Utah, the young, thrusting FBI agent determined to get ahead at all costs and Bodhi, the cool, laid-back, mystical surfer dude who also masterminds bank heists on the side. While he was a huge star in the '80s through such films as *Dirty Dancing*, *Road House* and *Ghost*, Patrick Swayze was determined to expand his acting opportunities in the '90s, so opted for a part in the Roland Joffe drama *City of Joy* and for the part of Bodhi, the supporting role in *Point Break*.

Carrying *Point Break* fell to Keanu Reeves, in his first stab at action-hero status. Talking to *Interview* magazine, Keanu was looking forward to taking on an action role, something that had not been available to the young actor previously in his career. 'The character is a kind of adrenalin junkie, and there's this other adrenalin

Keanu as FBI agent Johnny Utah and Patrick Swayze as laid-back surfer dude Bodhi in Point Break.

junkie [Swayze] and they push each other into jumping out of aeroplanes, shooting guns, shit like that.'

Keanu took his role seriously, getting into the background of his FBI character and also physically training for what he knew would be a punishing film shoot. 'I've been hanging out with athletes, FBI agents, police, people in college fraternities. I'm seeing a whole other part of the world, y'know.' As well as spending time with real FBI agents, Keanu also learned how to handle firearms at LAPD's target range, and practised football training with the UCLA quarterback coaches, to get the right background for Johnny Utah, an ex-football hero before he became an FBI agent.

Said Keanu: 'As *Point Break* begins, Johnny Utah is a very physical, very competitive, very cocky character who's not sure if he's ever really been happy. He has always liked living on the edge, but through his relationship with Bodhi, he learns a lot about himself.'

Keanu's physical flexibility helped him out greatly when he took up surfing lessons shortly after beginning discussions with Bigelow about starring in *Point Break*. 'The first time I went into the water, the board just smacked me in the head! But eventually I could do it, I could stand up, depending on the wave. It was a kind of a small summer, wave-wise, but some of the waves you see me on – that's me, yeah.' It was just as well for Keanu that his character was an undercover cop and so was not meant to be that proficient at surfing, as he learned just enough to fake it and get by.

For Keanu playing Johnny Utah meant not only learning to surf, but also how to fire a gun and jump out of aeroplanes – a real crash course in action film-making. Despite the role having been offered to both Swayze and Matthew Broderick, director Kathryn Bigelow reckoned that Keanu was ready for action. 'I've been an enormous fan of Keanu since *River's Edge*,' said Bigelow. 'When this film came up, I thought Keanu's innate physicality, intelligence and charm would make him perfect to play Utah. He holds the screen, and he's got a magical ability to put the audience in his back pocket. In addition, the role was a departure from the work he'd done in the past. We all felt it would be a fresh approach for the picture.'

Keanu was allowed to take part in all the action, with the exception of the sky-diving. Despite being keen to follow through with the action sequences, the insurers of the film raised objections to having the star fall out of an aeroplane. 'The money aspect of the film was very concerned about twisted ankles and death,' noted Keanu, as he carried out his sky-diving scenes held by cables and on a series of moving platforms. Only Swayze actually did any sky-diving, and then only after all filming was finished.

For Keanu playing Johnny Utah meant not only learning how to surf, but also how to jump out of aeroplanes and handle a gun.

Keanu takes time out with Lori Petty, the only woman in Point Break.

Production began on 9 July 1990 and ran for a gruelling 77 days, three years after the idea for the film had first been developed. For the film's surfing sequences, the film crew utilised Southern California beaches, heading as far north as Ventura County and as far south as Manhattan Beach. Key scenes were also shot in Hawaii, at Oahu's north shore, site of the Bansai Pipeline. For Keanu, the trip was a spiritual return home. For the spectacular sky-diving sequences, the crew set up residence at several airstrips by Edward's Air Force Base in Palmdale, California and at Lake Powell in Arizona.

When the film was released, *Empire* magazine got more excited about the new, hunky Keanu Reeves than almost anything else in *Point Break*, calling it 'a spiritual action picture. . .Keanu Reeves, who is maturing ve-ry nice-ly, girls, is eager beaver FBI recruit Johnny Utah, young, dumb and full of cum . . .'

British critics had their own problems with Bigelow's film. 'Keanu Reeves's boring cocky FBI agent goes undercover and off the film lurches into narrative gobbledygook, surfing and the spiritual utterances of a tanned guru (Swayze)' wrote Geoff Brown in *The Times*. The *Guardian* wondered aloud: 'A great deal of male bonding goes on in between the stunts and one occasionally wonders what a woman is doing shooting it so lovingly.'

Critically slammed, *Point Break* nonetheless went on to become one of the biggest summer hits of 1991, and the movie successfully launched a new image for Keanu Reeves, that of action hero. Now he'd fulfilled audience perceptions of him as something of a hunk by playing a role in which he played up his macho maleness.

There was little of the fey, almost androgynous nature of some of his teen movie roles in *Point Break*. Here he was all man – which, ironically, served to draw Keanu a considerable gay following, who read more into the film than may have been intended.

Some of the reviews of *Point Break* had noted a homoerotic subtext in the film between the characters of Johnny Utah and Bodhi. It was an angle the film-makers were keen to play down – and despite Keanu's relationship with Lori Petty in the film, it was nevertheless open to that interpretation.

Keanu's character of Johnny Utah had two mentors in the film – his ageing FBI partner Pappas (Gary Busey) and surfer guru Bodhi (Swayze). These male relationships were at the heart of the film, which at times seemed to become little more than a celebration of the male physique in action – whether rubber-clad surfers or macho sky-divers. Utah's initial connection with Tyler (Petty) is based on a falsehood when he misleads her to get closer to Bodhi, captivated as he is by his display of agility on his surf board. At one stage, Petty's Tyler storms off from the macho gang commenting: 'too much testosterone here'.

Being two sides of the same character, the attraction between Utah and Bodhi is played up. When Utah has a chance to shoot Bodhi (clad in his Reagan mask), he deliberately shoots into the air instead. Forced to take part in a bank robbery, Utah comments, 'I can't do this', only for Bodhi to retort: 'You might like it'. Dialogue like that – and Bodhi's line to Utah 'You want me so bad it's like acid in your mouth' – all backed up the homoerotic style of the shooting. Utah's obsession with Bodhi has him track the fugitive to Australia, where Bodhi gives in 'just for you'.

The sexuality of *Point Break* may have been a matter of debate, but there was no doubt about the next, risky film which Keanu Reeves was to opt for.

A pet project of independent, gay American film-maker Gus Van Sant, *My Own Private Idaho* (1991) was an unlikely film in which two of Hollywood's leading heart-throbs of the late '80s/early '90s would be expected to appear.

Keanu and River Phoenix get up close and personal in My Own Private Idaho.

Keanu keeps busy, going from Point Break *to* My Own Private Idaho *and* Little Buddha.

From a fairly privileged background, Van Sant was fascinated by America's street life. That interest had inspired two previous films, *Mala Noche* (1985) about a cross-racial romance between a grocery clerk and a Mexican migrant worker, and *Drugstore Cowboy* (1989), which featured an acclaimed performance from Matt Dillon as the leader of a group of drug addicts who raided drug stores for illicit supplies. Van Sant had been the recipient of several awards for *Drugstore Cowboy*, including the 1989 Society of Film Critics Award for Best Film, Best Director and Best Screenplay. The success of the film had propelled Van Sant to the forefront of independent film-makers – someone whom many actors were keen to work with.

Van Sant had his next project ready, a script examining the lowlife world of street hustlers. Entitled *My Own Private Idaho,* the title was lifted from a song by cult band the B-52s. Although the story of narcoleptic street kid Mike Waters and slumming rich kid Scott Favor was an original, Van Sant had drawn inspiration for some aspects of the story from Shakespeare's *Henry IV,* parts one and two.

The only way Van Sant saw of getting his film made was to cast unknowns in the two leading roles, but he did have a dream cast in mind – River Phoenix as Mike and Keanu Reeves as Scott. 'I just assumed their agents would say "no",' recalled Van Sant of his decision to send copies of the script to the two young heart-throb actors.

The script focused on the quest of male prostitute Mike (Phoenix) for his missing mother, a task hindered by his narcolepsy, a condition which causes him to fall into a coma-like stupor when under stress. Involved with Mike on the quest is Scott Favor, a modern Prince Hal, who is running from his inheritance of a fortune and responsibility from his harsh father. Scott is also the object of Mike's unreciprocated love.

Gus Van Sant saw *My Own Private Idaho* as 'the story of a rich boy who falls off the hill, and a kid on the street. I saw a bit of the hill in Keanu's personality and a bit of the street in River's. They played out these extensions of themselves.'

It was controversial material for the stars of *Stand by Me* (1986) and *Bill and Ted's Excellent Adventure* to even consider. Even the production company behind the film,

RIVER PHOENIX   KEANU REEVES

whatever
it takes
to have
a nice day.

my own private IDAHO ⑱

A FILM BY GUS VAN SANT

New Line Cinema (who had produced the hit horror *Nightmare on Elm Street* series of films), were having second thoughts about the project. The idea of casting Phoenix and Keanu, however, gave New Line a new interest in the film. 'As we began to talk to River and Keanu,' noted Van Sant, 'it was clear they were up for the challenge.'

For both actors *My Own Private Idaho* was a chance for them to escape their 'safe' teen idol images and branch out into more challenging work – a course both actors were very keen to take at this point in their lives. The script had been refused several times by Phoenix's long-time agent, Iris Burton, even denying her young client the opportunity to see it for himself. It was Keanu who, when visiting Phoenix, passed on a copy of Van Sant's script and raised the idea of them both starring in the film. Their youthful friendship and a sense of bravado resulted in the pair egging each other on to commit to the controversial parts in the film. 'Keanu and I made a kind of blood-brother pact,' admitted Phoenix. 'I can't imagine who else I would have done it with. We just forced ourselves into it. We said "Okay, I'll do it if you do it. I won't do it if you won't." We shook hands, that was it.'

Keanu saw the positive aspects of his role as more enticing than any worries his agent might express about the possibilities of damage to his career by playing the part. 'When I read it I realised it was just an amazing part,' recalled Keanu. 'It's a weird story, so I was just very happy to be there.' After all, Gus Van Sant had managed to draw out an acclaimed performance from Matt Dillon in *Drugstore Cowboy*, and Keanu – always willing to learn about his acting potential from his directors – hoped for a similar outcome from *My Own Private Idaho*.

'Keanu just said "Yeah, I'll do it", without having to think too much,' said Van Sant. 'River's nature made him more methodical about choosing any role. I would never want the responsibility of having talked them into it. I wanted their support so much.'

Throughout the drama of *My Own Private Idaho*, Keanu's Scott operates as Mike's protector, looking out for him when his lapses into unconsciousness render him vulnerable. Unlike Mike, though, Keanu's Scott is only on the streets temporarily, intending to return to the family fold upon turning 21 when he will inherit his fortune. His intention is to impress his peers with his switch from the lowlife world of sex-for-money to the circles of high finance and city politics (much the same thing, according to Van Sant). In a parody of Shakespeare's Prince Hal, he admits: 'It will impress them more, when such a fuck-up like me turns good.'

With no such escape on the horizon, Mike sets out on a trip to Rome in search of his long-lost mother, a journey Scott is willing to accompany him on, until he meets and falls in love with an Italian girl, turning his back on Mike in the end.

At the climax of the film comes two funerals – that of Scott's real father, the Mayor of Portland, and that of Mike's father-of-the-streets Bob Pigeon (William Richert). While the newly responsible Scott solemnly carries out his family duties with his new Italian wife, Mike and his street-gang pals are dancing on Bob's grave, before once more setting out on the road that never ends.

The film really belongs to River Phoenix, whose character has the audience sympathy, whereas Keanu turns out to be the bad guy, returning to the moneyed fold in the end. It was the first time in his career that Keanu had played a basically unsympathetic character. However, both young actors shone in a key scene about halfway through the film. Stuck in the middle of nowhere when their stolen motorbike breaks down, the pair are ensconced by a camp-fire when Mike begins to haltingly reveal his true feelings for Scott. While Phoenix emotes, Keanu freezes, unwilling to acknowledge his friend's feelings, and certainly desperate to avoid reciprocating. Phoenix and Keanu had worked out the staging of the scene themselves, with Phoenix in particular making the moment more important in the development of his character. For Keanu, filming parts of the project became an ordeal, recalling his *Wolfboy* days on stage in Toronto, six years previously at the beginning of his career. 'I'm not against gays or anything,' he said, 'but I won't have sex with guys. I would never do that on film. We did a little of it in *Idaho*, and – believe me – it was hard work. Never again.'

During the shooting of the camp-fire scene, River Phoenix had ribbed Keanu about playing a gay part, helpfully pointing out to him: 'Just think, Keanu – five hundred million of your fans will be watching this one day!' The comment was enough to throw Keanu off his stride, resulting in a strong reprimand for Phoenix from Van Sant, while Keanu recovered his composure enough to finish shooting the scene.

Phoenix and Keanu took their research seriously, hanging out with real street hustlers to tune into the lifestyle of the roles they were to play. It was research that nearly got the pair caught up in a potentially nasty incident in Los Angeles when they were confronted by groups of knife-wielding gang members. 'We'd accidentally wandered into the no man's land between two street gangs. They thought we were invading their territory. It suddenly got very heavy. Both gangs thought we were trying to work their territory,' recalled Keanu of the confrontation. 'It was terrifying – and there was no way we could tell them we were actors, they'd have cut us to pieces. We pretended we were ordinary guys – and then ran like hell!'

As well as the controversial sex aspects of the film, *My Own Private Idaho* featured drug-taking as central to its characters' lives. For River Phoenix, his method-like research for the part resulted in a real-life drug addiction that was to contribute heavily to his untimely early death in 1993. For Keanu Reeves, it recalled his earlier drug experience when he first arrived in Los Angeles. 'I dug it,' said Keanu, of taking drugs. 'I'm glad I hallucinated in my life.' Keanu had freely admitted to the availability of hash and LSD during his schooldays, and he'd certainly dabbled in drugs on and off himself. In an admission to *Interview* magazine he stated: 'I want to be on speed! I've never been on speed. I want to be a speed freak for a while. Is that a stupid thing to say?'

During the filming of *My Own Private Idaho* it appeared that the two young stars, as well as the real street kids who featured in the film and musicians like Flea from Red Hot Chili Peppers, were involved in taking drugs. 'There were rumours of people using heroin on that movie,' confirmed Mickey Cottrell, publicist for *My Own Private Idaho*, 'but I was there and I didn't see anything.' However, *Premiere* magazine correspondent Ralph Rogoff had a different impression of life during the making of the film. 'Having recently bought a large house, [Van Sant] invited several of the street kids in the cast to use it as a crash pad. Phoenix and Keanu moved in shortly afterward, and the place soon took on the aspect of a rock 'n' roll dormitory, with futons spread out on the floor and guitar jam sessions lasting through the night. Van Sant, in need of time alone, ended up retreating to a downtown loft.'

The conditions were right, according to Rugoff, for the participants to take their research too far in the area of drugs. One of the street kid actors was even more forthcoming to *Spin* magazine: 'Everyone was getting high. It was the nature of the film. Some of these guys have been through this before, and as soon as filming was

During the shooting of Idaho *River and Keanu spent time hanging out with real street hustlers.*

over, they gave it up and got back to their work. This was the first time for River though, and he just went wild.'

While for River – not being chaperoned on set by his parents – the access to drugs was new, Keanu had experienced narcotics and seemed to approach them with a more mature attitude. He finished the film in 1991, and stopped taking the drugs that had been available on the set. It was something he was not to give much thought to again until, on the night of 31 October 1993, he was to hear of River's tragic death on the sidewalk of Sunset Boulevard.

For some critics, Keanu seemed to be somewhat uneasy in his role in *My Own Private Idaho*. His 'controversial performance', according to *Vanity Fair* had 'raised more than a few painted eyebrows'. The *Village Voice* noted that 'Reeves stands, or occasionally struts, uneasily. . .' More striking in its criticism was *Variety*, pointing out that 'The Shakespearean side of the story falls short due to Reeves's very narrow range as an actor.' Most of the accolades went to River Phoenix, who went on to win the Best Actor Award at the Venice Film Festival in September 1991.

The film raised the spectre of Keanu's sexuality once again, compounded by his appearance in a photo spread in *Vanity Fair* in October 1991 which showed the actor dressed as a Japanese geisha. His advisers were as perturbed by his willingness to have his ethnicity emphasised as they were by the questions it raised about his sexuality. Even in promoting the movie, Keanu seemed determined not to toe the party line. Appearing on stage with Phoenix at the New York Film Festival, both actors appeared something the worse for drink, seemingly totally uninterested in the press conference to the extent that Keanu leaned back, yawned loudly, then spat on the hall floor. Keanu was often seen to dislike promoting his films and dealing with the press. Laurie Parker, producer of *My Own Private Idaho*, noted: 'Keanu is normally reticent about the publicity and can be rude – in fact, he offends people all the time, and that's caused him to develop a weird rap in the press because, I think, he doesn't like to promote himself, but he was a joy to work with.'

Keanu quickly put *Point Break* and *My Own Private Idaho* behind him, having felt the roles had achieved his aim. 'Every actor has his own battles,' he told *Movieline* magazine, 'and mine right now is coming from a younger man trying to get more mature parts in cool films.' Keanu seemed determined to enjoy his freedom while it lasted, as the economics of being a film star were about to catch up with the actor once again.

After his experience of independent film, Keanu Reeves was ready to follow his manager's advice with a return to a tried-and-true successful concept – a sequel to *Bill and Ted's Excellent Adventure*. After the sleeper success of the original film in 1989, it seemed inevitable that the prospect of a sequel would be raised sooner or later.

The problem for Kroopf was going to be reuniting Alex Winter and Keanu Reeves from the first film for the sequel – provisionally entitled *Bill and Ted Go to Hell*. 'Their careers have moved on and they've grown up, so they were concerned that they not be locked into playing these two teenage characters. We said Bill and Ted can grow five years older, because the comic spark between them is not a particularly youth-

Going to hell: it was back to playing Ted for Keanu.

Together again: Alex Winter and Keanu play Bill and Ted one last time.

oriented thing. They're classic clowns, like Abbott and Costello, or Laurel and Hardy, and they should go on having adventures until they are senior citizens.'

That concern was particularly strongly felt by Keanu, who'd been acting well short of his actual age in many roles, from his teen-film days. To have Bill and Ted age in the sequel, as the actors had done in real life, was undoubtedly part of the attraction for Keanu. 'We have real jobs,' he said of the older, but no wiser Bill and Ted. 'We have our own place, we have our girlfriends and we're not in school. Bill is more frustrated and yet he's still hopeful and sincere in his goal: to be the best rock 'n' roll guitar player he can be, despite the fact that he has no ability whatsoever. Ted is more go-with-the-flow, but Bill really does struggle to get the band off the ground. He lives every day with the fact that they are really awful.'

Reteaming with Alex Winter was also a plus point for Keanu. In tackling films like *Point Break* and *My Own Private Idaho*, he was trying to stretch himself and change his public image at one and the same time. Perhaps to do Ted again would be a step backwards – but the need for a solid commercial hit film and the prospect of having a good time on the set won Keanu over.

The studio funding the new film were not keen on the writers' idea of sending the main characters to Hell. Orion executives asked Chris Matheson and Ed Solomon to develop a script for *Bill and Ted 2* based on the notion of Bill and Ted encountering characters from fiction. Not keen on this concept, the writers decided to enlist the star actors on their side. 'We knew Alex and Keanu didn't want to do the same thing over again,' confirmed Matheson, 'so we pitched our [Hell] idea to them. They really liked it, and told Orion that was the one they wanted to do.'

Keanu, although initially resistant to returning to the airhead role of Theodore 'Ted' Logan, which had done much to secure the image of the actor in the minds of so many, decided to go with the flow. 'I went through a phase of that self-consciousness a little bit, cos I'm kinda goofy, right? So I got over it, and now I'm just hopeless.'

Production on the project began on 7 January 1991 for a ten-week shooting period in the Santa Clarita studio complex in Valencia, California, about an hour north of Hollywood. There was a summer release date of 19 July already firmly pencilled in.

The expanded surreal project aimed to top the first movie, which was a relatively straightforward time travel adventure. Cast alongside Alex Winter and Keanu Reeves were Joss Ackland as the chief bad guy and William Sadler as Death, out to harvest Bill and Ted's souls.

'When we go to Hell,' said Keanu, 'Beelzebub sends us down into the tunnels of Hades, and we're confronted by our own particular nightmares. My nightmare is that when I was ten years old, I took my brother's Easter basket, so now I'm haunted by the Easter Bunny.'

Getting back into the part was easy for Keanu, according to director Peter Hewitt, who noted that Winter and Keanu 'know these characters incredibly well. My job with them more often than not is to just sit there and laugh at what they're doing,

With Gary Oldman in Bram Stoker's Dracula.

and occasionally suggest things. Ordinarily, they'll chat amongst themselves and come up with great stuff. It was fun to work with them.'

Despite Hewitt's on-the-record stance, it seems clear that whatever else Keanu was on the set of *Bogus Journey*, fun to work with was not one of them. Having come to *Bill and Ted* straight from filming *My Own Private Idaho*, Keanu had not quite shaken off the remnants of his previous persona. His behaviour on set was not always appreciated by those around him, and Keanu seemed unaware that turning up late and disappearing at odd times was an inconvenience for such a tightly scheduled production.

During shooting this seeming 'exhaustion' caught up with the actor, when he collapsed on set and was rushed semi-conscious to a Los Angeles hospital. Reports emanated that Keanu had been struck down by a 'mystery infection', and a source on set confirmed: 'It wasn't too serious and he was soon back at work.' However, industry speculation had Keanu readopting his teenage drug habits following his experiences on the set of *My Own Private Idaho*. Reports indicated he was having a nasty time of it. 'I got into drugs at eighteen,' Keanu had admitted, 'but nowadays, I'd say I was more of a motorcycle junkie.'

After production was wrapped it became clear that a title change for the film would be in order. As newspapers, TV and radio would not carry advertisements for the *Go To Hell* title, and *Bill and Ted 2* seemed somewhat unimaginative, the crew settled on *Bill and Ted's Bogus Journey* .

After filming was over, Keanu began to realise that he really had tired of the Bill and Ted concept. The new film was not the fun little movie that the first had been, but much more of a franchise product with a lot of money riding on it. Not only that, but the films had spawned a whole merchandising industry, ranging from Bill and Ted dolls to breakfast cereal. 'The doll sucks,' said Keanu, 'it's kind of crass, but the cereal's a good chew.'

The *Village Voice* was positive and thought *Bill and Ted's Bogus Journey* was 'a self-perpetuating, self-referential hit . . . make me eat a box of Bill and Ted's Excellent Cereal if these two knuckleheads don't win your heart a second time.'

Overall, Keanu was disappointed by the corporate mentality which now surrounded Bill and Ted. 'I saw a TV commercial where Ted was saying Bill's line and Bill was saying Ted's line! It's like they [the producers] didn't know the difference between them. Bill and Ted is a very specific mind-set to get into, and you can't just jump into that.'

Having gone straight from shooting his action-adventure heroics in *Point Break* in July 1990, then adopting the role of gay hustler Scott Favor in *My Own Private Idaho* in September, no one would have blamed Keanu for wanting to take a back seat after wrapping the shooting of *Bill and Ted's Bogus Journey* in the first half of 1991. It was not to be, though, as the actor plunged straight into another high profile role.

When Francis Ford Coppola set out to make a new version of the oft-told tale of *Dracula* he had one overall aim in mind – a faithful adaptation of the original source novel, something the director felt had never been achieved before on film. With that in mind, Coppola entitled his latest film project *Bram Stoker's Dracula*.

It was actress Winona Ryder who had drawn Coppola's attention to the screenplay for the film by James V. Hart, then entitled *Dracula: the Untold Story*.

Winona Ryder as Mina and Keanu as Jonathan Harker in Bram Stoker's Dracula.

Attracted by its faithfulness to the book, Coppola's concern was with the budget. The studio, Columbia, wanted a $30 million film ready for a November 1992 release. Known for budget-busting films like *One From The Heart* (1984), Coppola took a radical decision on how to achieve the film within the financial limits set. 'I said, how about we do it all in the studio with hanging miniatures, do everything in a style like the old days,' said Coppola. 'Since *Dracula* is set around 1897, we used the tricks of the early magicians when they first started experimenting with film . . . I liked the idea of making a turn-of-the-century movie.'

Casting became Coppola's next concern. With Ryder already attached to the film as Mina, Coppola followed the actress's suggestion of Anthony Hopkins as vampire hunter Van Helsing. Filling the title role proved a harder task. 'In general, our concept was to use a young cast,' said Coppola. 'I felt that Gary Oldman had the passion. He's young, so he could do the romantic parts.'

The pivotal role of Jonathan Harker, the narrator of Stoker's book and the central audience-identification character in the film, remained to be filled. The role of the Englishman who journeys to Carpathia on legal business to meet Count Dracula and gets caught up in the Count's bizarre world did not seem like ideal material for Keanu Reeves, the man who for many audiences was Ted Logan. 'I was just hired on the strength of Winona Ryder putting me forward for the part,' revealed Keanu of his casting in *Bram Stoker's Dracula*. 'The director didn't really know my work, but he'd been told that I was popular with younger people.' Once Keanu had met and worked with Coppola he became a confirmed fan of his director. 'He's a man of many, many ideas and a man who sets up a creative situation where you can explore.'

In supporting roles, Coppola cast Cary Elwes as Arthur Holmwood, Sadie Frost as Lucy Westenra, *Withnail and I* actor Richard E. Grant as Dr Seward and *Rocketeer* star Bill Campbell as Quincy Morris.

KEANU REEVES – AN EXCELLENT ADVENTURE

Bram Stoker's Dracula was to be a challenging film for all involved. While Keanu Reeves was struggling with his dialect coach to perfect his elusive English accent for the part of Harker, director Coppola was reinterpreting the script in a manner which would make it all producible within the confines of the studio walls.

One decision the director took was to showcase his young, attractive cast, rather than spend a fortune on gargantuan sets, as had been done in the recent *Batman* feature films. 'Since we had these beautiful young actors, and they were going to be our jewels that we were offering, I thought it would be interesting if we emphasised the costumes and not the sets,' said Coppola. To achieve his aims in the costumes, Coppola took the unusual step of hiring Japanese conceptual artist Eiko Ishioka to design the outfits for the cast of this youth-appeal *Dracula.*

Shooting began on Stage 30 of the Sony/Columbia studio lot in Culver City, Los Angeles – what had once been the old MGM backlot where film history had been made for over 60 years. With the entire film shot on sound stages, except for two days of London street exteriors, using the Universal backlot, *Bram Stoker's Dracula* had occupied all seven sound stages and used over 60 individual sets. With a two-week break over Christmas, shooting concluded on schedule on 31 January 1992.

There were tensions behind the scenes on *Bram Stoker's Dracula* which served to make everyone's job that much harder. Lead actor Gary Oldman was suffering from an allergic reaction to his copious foam rubber make-up, and his foul moods on set often resulted in arguments with Coppola as well as with other cast members, such as Winona Ryder. During the production Oldman was arrested for driving under the influence and suffered a six-month driving ban and community service. Keanu wasn't having a great time either; having come straight onto *Dracula* from the excesses of *My Own Private Idaho* and the pressured set of *Bill and Ted's Bogus Journey*, he was exhausted.

The whole movie was turned by Coppola into a low-tech special effects extravaganza, with even sequences that seemed not to be obvious set pieces being enhanced by Coppola's unique approach. One such scene was when Keanu's Jonathan Harker encounters the three vampire brides of Dracula in the castle. 'We worked very hard on the sensuous scene with Harker and the brides,' recalled floor effects supervisor Michael Lantieri, who used tricks such as trap doors and hidden air tubes to bring an unsettling weirdness to the scene. Other scenes, such as the one where Dracula physically picks up the waiting Harker and puts him in his horse-drawn coach, are given a bizarre ambience thanks to the strange in-camera effects Coppola and his crew achieved on the film.

Arguably the finished product bore little resemblance to some of the ideas that Coppola had floated in public. It's as though they were testing the waters before deciding how far to take things in the film. According to supposed 'reports from the set' the film would contain 'explicit sex, rampant bestiality and horrifying scenes of blood and gore'. James V. Hart joined in the charade: 'Dracula can make people commit sexual acts beyond their own imaginations – and well beyond what society would permit.'

Bram Stoker's Dracula out-performed most industry expectations, becoming something of an unexpected hit. It seemed audiences were ready for a new retelling of the Dracula tale, a modern version with young stars and an experimental vibe, which emphasised the dark romance of the story.

The film had a dramatic impact. The retro-style special effects gave the entire enterprise an eerie and unusual feel, ideally suited to the material. However, this

sense of style was achieved at some expense. The performances varied wildly and the story lacked drive in places. Despite this there were many pleasures to be drawn from the film, even including some of the eccentric performances. Unfortunately, many people, including Keanu Reeves himself, agreed that he simply had been miscast in the central role of Jonathan Harker. He couldn't handle the accent required, no matter how hard he tried, and he was simply not convincing as the pawn of Dracula or the lust object for the trio of undead Brides. It was the first major misfire in the actor's career.

For J. Hoberman in the *Village Voice*, Keanu was decidedly out-of-place. 'As the ill-fated Harker, Keanu is so wanly out of it he seems to have had his blood drained already. Small wonder that his prim fiancée Mina (Winona Ryder) falls for Dracula when he arrives in London.' Veteran American film critic Stanley Kaufman commented: '[Keanu] behaves like a quite nice high school boy in the senior class production of *Dracula*.' Again the actor's youthful looks had got in the way of a critic taking one of his performances seriously.

Hostile criticism of Keanu's performances, like those in *Bram Stoker's Dracula* and his later film *Little Buddha*, served to hold the actor back from fully exploring his potential. 'I feel like I'm just beginning,' was Keanu's attitude to these kind of reviews. 'I've had some success and some failures. I got killed in *Dracula* – I got slaughtered. The other actors' performances were so operatic, and I didn't hold up my end of the bargain. My performance was too introverted, closed in and safe. Since *Dracula* came out I've always felt that I could have played it much more aggressive . . . I didn't act very well. I'll leave it at that.'

Keen to put a positive spin on even the worst criticism, Keanu knew that he was learning on the job and could still go some way to improve his acting. But being a less than perfect thespian was not going to affect his star status – whatever accent he tried. 'I didn't think the accent [in *Dracula*] was that bad, but supposedly it was. Since I've stunk in some films, I guess I have something to prove. . .'

Whether Keanu Reeves had something to prove to critics in terms of his acting abilities, he was sure of one thing. His recent films had secured and expanded a growing fan base, as he moved from being an obscure teen actor with an oddball name to one of Hollywood's A-list young actors, capable of diverse performances and willing, albeit not always successfully, to tackle out-of-the ordinary material – he allowed himself the right to fail, even if the critics did not. Both *Point Break* and *Bill and Ted's Bogus Journey* appealed directly to the young, mainly female, teen audience who had grown up with Keanu and his films. Similarly, *Point Break* and *My Own Private Idaho* put him firmly on the map as an icon and pin-up in the gay community, alongside his *Idaho* co-star River Phoenix. While Phoenix seemed happy to experiment with his sexuality on and off screen, the topic was something Keanu steered clear of, even though *Idaho* had revived some of the speculation which had dogged his stage debut in *Wolfboy*. The 'Is Keanu Gay?' rumour-mill was very soon to kick into overdrive, but the actor did himself no favours by not appearing to follow the up-front habits of most young, promiscuous Hollywood actors.

Tackled about his lack of visibility on the Hollywood social scene, Keanu put up what even he seemed to realise was a feeble defence. 'I'm a homebody. I don't get invited out much. In the past year I've just been doing these films, I haven't had much of a life. I do hang out with my friends, ride my motorcycle and listen to music.'

When it came down to relationships with women, Keanu just didn't seem to want to know. 'Sure, I've had no shortage of offers,' he insisted, 'but I prefer to channel my passions into bikes because they're cool, fast and less trouble.'

Such was Keanu Reeves' newly confirmed celebrity that he was invited to appear in a music video by singer Paula Abdul. Between films, Keanu donned the persona of James Dean – an experience he called 'another regurgitation of icons and culture by the American media' – for Abdul's 'Rush Rush' video. The song turned out to be the fastest selling of her career, no doubt helped by Keanu's presence in the video.

The music and film industry rumour-mill worked overtime with speculation that Abdul and Keanu had hit it off and become romantically involved. Asked about it all, Keanu was as evasive as ever. 'What can I say? It was an interesting experience. I met Paula Abdul at a charity event, and she's a very interesting lady. I think she dug my stuff, you know, so she approached me to do the video. I thought I might as well check it out.'

Although he got to mime playing guitar on the video, Keanu thought afterwards that his latent ambitions of playing in a band would have to wait. 'When I saw snatches of the video, I just thought, wow, man, you're not cool enough for that, so I guess I'm not going to be in any more videos.'

After the rumoured tryst with Abdul, Keanu was next linked with *Baywatch* babe Pamela Anderson. It was certainly an unlikely combination, and again Keanu came up with an evasive answer to journalists' questions. 'You show up at a première together and the next thing you know, they've got you married,' was Keanu's only comment on the reports that there may have been more going on between him and Anderson than he was willing to let on.

He did have strong views about having relationships with his co-stars. 'If you have relationships with the women you work with then you become part of the Hollywood gossip-mongers, and I try to stay out of all that. If you don't have relationships with the women you work with then people say you're gay. You're damned if you do and damned if you don't. It's easier to work with women if your relationship is professional and not romantic.'

Although interested in having a family at some point, Keanu had more materialistic desires at the forefront of his mind. 'I'd like maybe to get a boat some day, and sail around,' he said. 'Maybe I'll settle down and raise a family. I've always wanted kids.'

Before his personal life, though, came the work – and while he was getting plenty of offers, Keanu aimed to continue to take advantage of them. 'If I didn't get so many parts, then I wouldn't be working as much as I am. I'm very, very lucky. Most actors are lucky to get one good film every two years. I'm getting three and four films each year and they're good parts! I try hard, and I think that word has gotten around that I study for my parts. I've never been one of those actors that shows up on the set not knowing his lines. I always try to be the pro people expect.'

Keanu had certainly been on something of a ride, with *Point Break, My Own Private Idaho, Bill and Ted's Bogus Journey* and *Bram Stoker's Dracula* all under his belt in an amazingly short time. The diversity of his performances and of his directors set something of a pattern that Keanu would follow for a while yet, but for the moment he was happy to rest on his laurels and marvel at his achievements. 'One moment I'm playing the hero, and the next I'm the clown,' he said. 'I've certainly done a few films that are very different.'

CHAPTER SIX

Bard and Buddha

K EANU REEVES did emerge from his self-imposed sabbatical for one downright odd film. Back before the cameras in the spring of 1992, the last thing on Keanu's mind when filming *Freaked* (also known as *Hideous Mutant Freakz*) was furthering his career, buried as he was under half a ton of latex and hair, playing his most bizarre character to date: Ortiz the 'Dawg Boy', as proclaimed on an advertising billboard in the film. One attraction of this weird and wonderful project was the opportunity to work again with his *Bill and Ted* partner, Alex Winter, who was now writing and directing.

Winter had a film project underway, a black comic horror B-movie concerning a travelling band of circus freaks, mutated by a strange toxic fertiliser. Among the oddball characters in the movie were a bearded lady played by *The A-Team* star Mr T, a talk-show star played by Brooke Shields and an evil multi-national boss who dumps the toxic waste, played by William Sadler, Death in *Bill and Ted's Bogus Journey*. Studio 20th Century Fox agreed to finance Winter's bizarre movie, only if the *Bill and Ted* star agreed to play the leading part of Ricky, a one-time big movie star, now the show's leading freak. Winter reluctantly agreed, signing up Randy Quaid as the travelling circus's showman. There was in his performance as movie idol Ricky Coogan more than a hint of a send-up of his *Bill and Ted* co-star, Keanu Reeves.

For Keanu, it was hard to resist the chance to work with Winter again – and to play such an off-the-wall part. In the movie, Keanu is unrecognisable, his movie idol good looks smothered in latex and fur, a four-hour make-up application job. It was not the kind of appearance that his growing legion of teenage female fans would have expected of their idol – and that's all the justification Keanu needed to take on the role.

A riotous mix of political satire, scatological humour and bad taste antics, *Freaked* is ideal midnight-screening, cult movie material. It's perhaps a bit too knowing to succeed as a genuine cult movie, being too deliberately wacky for its own good. A re-edited version was released in America, removing several key scenes featuring Keanu, including a freak game show sequence. These scenes remained intact in the European video version.

With a change of regime at 20th Century Fox, *Freaked* was dumped as being too dark and unsuitable for mainstream audiences. It played for limited engagements in New York and Los Angeles in October 1993, but found a much more appreciative cult audience upon video release.

Keanu in disguise as Ortiz the Dawg Boy in Alex Winter's Freaked.

The appearance of Keanu Reeves in the film went uncredited on the cinema release, but was splashed all over the video sleeve as an inducement to buy or rent, even though the actor has relatively few scenes in the movie. *Freaked* was but a momentary diversion, an actor's indulgence – Keanu Reeves had bigger plans in mind for his future career. He was now to be more active in seeking out and securing unusual roles for himself, rather than sitting back and waiting for offers.

After the craziness of playing Ortiz the 'Dawg Boy', Keanu Reeves was about to return to what was his first love – playing Shakespeare, courtesy of British writer-director Kenneth Branagh. Keanu had heard that Branagh was in development of a film version of *Much Ado About Nothing*, and saw this as an ideal opportunity to play true Shakespeare on film, as opposed to the cod version utilised in *My Own Private Idaho* or the costume dramatics of *Dangerous Liaisons*. To that end, Keanu contacted Branagh, hoping for a role in the film of a play he knew well.

For Branagh, *Much Ado About Nothing*, Shakespeare's battle-of-the-sexes comedy, was a project close to his heart. 'The play is one of the greatest romantic comedies ever written,' explained the writer-director-star of *Henry V*. 'Like many of Shakespeare's comedies, it's very earthy and very lustful. My intention was to make explicit in the film what is only implicit in the play.'

In common with Stephen Frears when he tackled *Dangerous Liaisons* several years before, Branagh was well aware of the box office reasons for casting American actors in this European tale – even if he did offer an alternative justification for the casting. 'I've always admired American film actors for the emotional fearlessness they have. That's how I think you should deal with Shakespeare, that sort of blood-and-guts, high-octane approach.'

A romantic tale filmed by Branagh in the idyllic Tuscan countryside, *Much Ado About Nothing* has the return of soldiers from war as the catalyst for its comic complications. At the heart of the villainous plot that runs through the movie is Don John (Keanu), the bastard and jealous brother of victorious-in-love-and-battle Don Pedro (Denzel Washington).

'I had seen *Henry V* and enjoyed it, but I did not really take note of who created it and why,' recalled Keanu of his first encounter with Kenneth Branagh. 'When I went to meet him, my enthusiasm grew. I love Shakespeare and I love to act in Shakespeare, and in speaking with Ken and watching the film [*Henry V*] I was very enthusiastic and very happy to be there. I felt lucky and glad.'

Playing the villain was not something Keanu was very used to, his nearest comparison being the anti-hero role of Scott Favor in *My Own Private Idaho. Much Ado About Nothing* was to be something very different. '[Don John] is an unresolved character. I come in as a malcontent, I leave as a malcontent. We just wanted Don John to be a physical threat and a man of action.'

The challenge for Keanu Reeves on *Much Ado About Nothing* was handling the Shakespearean dialogue, and trying to ensure it didn't come across like *Bill and Ted* surfer-dude-speak, as was the case (to varying degrees) in *Dangerous Liaisons, Bram Stoker's Dracula* and later in *Little Buddha.* 'You have to say the line over

Keanu indulging his love of Shakespeare in Much Ado About Nothing.

'Keanu has an aloof quality,' said Kenneth Branagh of his star, 'a far-away quality. You can't quite get close to him.'

and over, so that you have physical speech clarity and clarity of thought. I call it a convergence into what language really is, which is manufacturing sound to express a psycho-emotional need.'

Working closely with Keanu on his accent and approach to Shakespeare's lines on *Much Ado About Nothing* was voice coach Russell Jackson. Aware of the seeming inability of American actors to capture British accents, Jackson and Branagh decided to side-step the problem. 'It was decided from the outset that the Americans would not pretend to have British accents, or the strange stage-Shakespearean that used to be common in America,' confirmed Jackson. 'That would alienate audiences and make the actors feel constrained. We wanted the feeling of natural voices.'

For his part, Kenneth Branagh saw Keanu's Don John very clearly: 'Truly malevolent, sexy, passionate, an obsessively evil creature. In leather trousers. Pretty tight – I'd pay money to see Keanu Reeves in leather trousers and I think a lot of other people would as well.'

Principal photography on *Much Ado About Nothing* began in Tuscany in August 1992. With temperatures reaching 100 degrees, the location looked wonderful on screen, but the cast and crew suffered in the heat in their efforts to get the project on film. The schedule was tight, with only seven weeks allocated for the location shoot in the idyllic setting of the 14th-century Villa Vignamaggio, overlooking the town of Greve, centre of the Chianti wine region.

Seen as part of Britain's habit of 'heritage' film-making, *Much Ado About Nothing* was broadly welcomed, although many critics seemed to feel that Branagh had taken a far too sunny approach to material which did contain at its heart a darker undercurrent. Again, as part of a large ensemble cast, Keanu Reeves's unexpected presence was often noted. According to the *Village Voice*, 'a scowling Keanu stalks the periphery'. Roger Ebert, writing in the *Chicago Sun-Times*, agreed: 'Don John, wearing a wicked black beard, mopes about the edges of the screen, casting dark looks upon the merrymakers.' British critic Iain Johnstone, in the *Sunday Times*, noted: 'Keanu Reeves is only able to avail himself of two expressions – brood and sneer – but, boy, does the camera love this actor . . .'

For Kenneth Branagh, the appeal of Keanu Reeves is timeless. 'Keanu has an aloof quality,' he said of his co-star, 'a far-away quality. You can't quite get close to him, he is somehow unattainable. That makes him very, very attractive. Yet, he seems to display all the qualities one would want: a very sexy, erotic physical being. One sees in his work that he can sometimes be very gentle, he can sometimes be very fierce, he can sometimes be very funny, And yet, he's got something at the back of the eyes that says, "No, I won't be committing here." He'll always be on the bus, heading off. And I think there is something tremendously attractive to men and women about the combination of the utterly desirable and the definitely unattainable.'

Having succeeded in putting himself forward for a role in *Much Ado About Nothing*, Keanu repeated the trick when he saw a chance to work with *My Own Private Idaho* director Gus Van Sant again, on his proposed film version of Tom Robbins's 1970s cult novel *Even Cowgirls Get the Blues*.

The incident-laden story follows the unusual adventures of Sissy Hankshaw (Uma Thurman), a lanky girl cursed with extra large thumbs. Naturally, she becomes the

Keanu plays Don John the bastard and jealous brother of Don Pedro (Denzel Washington).

Keanu as Julian in Even Cowgirls Get the Blues.

world's greatest hitchhiker. At various points in the story she finds herself as a model for the New York social doyenne known only as The Countess (John Hurt) and his feminine hygiene products; part of a circle of Warholian drop-outs and artists in New York, including Julian, an educated full-blooded Mohawk Indian (Keanu Reeves); and eventually ending up in an affair with Bonanza Jellybean (Rain Phoenix, sister of River) at her all-female Rubber Rose Ranch health spa, which is being held under siege.

Gus Van Sant had first read the book in the 1970s. 'I really liked it, and it was something I've wanted to film ever since then, though until recently I had no way to really do it.' Van Sant eventually met up with author Robbins. 'I was absolutely delighted,' recalled Robbins, 'because I had seen *Drugstore Cowboy* and realised that this man is a real artist.'

Keanu had been recruited by Van Sant at a party over a year before production began. Keanu had already read the book and suggested himself to Van Sant for the part of Julian. Casting the role of the second-generation American Indian had been proving a problem for Van Sant – and here was the answer presenting himself. For Keanu's part, the film couldn't have been more offbeat, different from his other work and unexpected – just the qualities that no doubt piqued his interest in the first place.

Keanu was keen to be working with Van Sant again, even if only in a limited role. 'I'm very interested in becoming a better actor,' he claimed. 'I'd like to do a lot of different things. That's the challenge, the test, the scary part and also the interesting aspect of acting.'

Heavily criticised at both Cannes and Toronto Film Festivals, the release of *Even Cowgirls Get the Blues* was delayed in America while Van Sant re-edited the film, hoping to make it more accessible to audiences. The result was that Keanu's already cameo-sized role was reduced still further, something which pleased the actor when he realised what a turkey the movie had turned out to be. A single scene cameo by his friend River Phoenix was cut out altogether, as the film was eventually released after his death from a drug overdose. It seems the irony of dedicating a film to Phoenix in which drug-taking is celebrated escaped Gus Van Sant, the director whose work with Phoenix on *My Own Private Idaho*, probably more than anything else, contributed towards the actor's tragically premature death.

The critics seemed to take pleasure in mauling the film, with even the *Village Voice* attacking its incompetence. 'Van Sant deranges the novel's eccentricities with his own. Wholesome and trippy, basically an increasingly dull series of riffs against an intermittently busy background . . . Thurman's nominal co-star Keanu Reeves was largely edited out even before the movie's less than epochal Toronto première.' British writers were equally scathing, calling the film an 'epic whimsy' in the *Financial Times*, 'a mess' in the *Guardian* and 'an embarrassing miscalculation' by *Time Out*.

After playing roles as diverse as airhead Ted in *Bill and Ted's Excellent Adventure*, tough FBI agent Johnny Utah in *Point Break*, slumming rich kid Scott Favor in *My Own Private Idaho* and even Jonathan Harker in *Bram Stoker's Dracula*, it still came as a surprise to most people when Keanu Reeves's name became attached to the role of Prince Siddhartha in *Little Buddha*. Could the now 29-year-old actor, best known for playing teenage goofballs, really be the right person to play Siddhartha, the 6th-century BC Indian Prince who became the Buddha?

As in the past with Stephen Frears, Lawrence Kasdan, Gus Vant Sant and most recently Francis Ford Coppola, Keanu found himself being selected by an acclaimed director for a major role. This time it was Bernardo Bertolucci, director of *Last Tango in Paris*, *The Spider's Stratagem* and *The Conformist*, as well as *The Last Emperor*, who saw in Keanu's almost Asian beauty the face he needed for Siddhartha.

Bertolucci himself was not a Buddhist, although he did have an audience with the Dalai Lama before embarking on the film. 'I told him I wasn't a Buddhist,' recalled Bertolucci. '"Ah, that's much better," he said. What I came out with was a feeling of great kindness and compassion.'

Having searched for four months for someone to play Siddhartha, Bertolucci had travelled to India hoping to find someone in an amateur theatre group who might be suitable for the part. He initially offered the role to famous 'Bollywood' actor Rahul Roy, who turned down the chance to make his Hollywood debut. According to *Spice* magazine, Roy was taking into account potential local reaction to Bertolucci's project in making his decision. Controversy continued as to whether Siddhartha had lived in Nepal or India. With Nepal having been choosen for filming, Roy felt that Indian film-makers would not approve. He was forced into politely, but firmly, turning down the offer.

Having recently seen *My Own Private Idaho* and noted Keanu's Canadian-Hawaiian origins in a magazine article, Bertolucci felt his desperation to fill the role had been answered.

Bertolucci arranged a meeting with Keanu in a hotel off New York's Central Park South – and Keanu turned up wearing a suit and tie; something he never usually did, but which showed his keenness to win the part. There was no doubt in Bertolucci's mind that, although the young actor was a daring choice, he had the right qualities for the role. 'Siddhartha was innocent and Keanu convinced me he could be that person,' recalled Bertolucci. Two further meetings were required – this time in Rome – before Bertolucci finally offered the part to Keanu.

The news of Keanu's casting was welcomed by the film's producer Jeremy Thomas, who was only too aware of the young actor's box office appeal. 'After all,' he candidly admitted, 'you want as many people as possible to see the film . . .'

Casting Keanu was an audacious move by Bertolucci, who became aware during shooting that some members of the crew had unkindly dubbed his film *Sid and Ted's Excellent Adventure*. For his part Keanu was defensive about his past work: 'Surf-boy films are not all I've done. I asked him [Bertolucci] why he'd picked me, and he said because of my innocence.'

There was a moment of disbelief on the actor's part, however, when Keanu was finally offered the role by Bertolucci. 'I was surprised, definitely. There was about eight minutes of feeling that "This is very audacious." But in the end that disappears and you're like, "Great, let's begin." But I had lots of people saying, "You can't play this part. . ."'

Keanu found a karmic reassurance that he was, indeed, the right man for the job. 'I'm 29. Siddhartha was 29 when he began his quest, so I'm historically, traditionally in my life at the beginning of the quest for spirituality.'

In the film, Chris Isaak and Bridget Fonda star as the parents of a young American child (Alex Wiesendanger) whom some Tibetans believe could be the reincarnation of a high lama. Along with their son, the pair investigate the trappings of Buddhism, and the tale of the enlightenment of Siddhartha, the Indian Prince who renounces worldly pleasures and religious extremism to find the Middle Way of Buddhist truth.

'I'm acting,' insisted Keanu of his spaced-out portrayal of Siddhartha. 'I had no exposure to Buddhism. All I knew about Buddha was that he was a smiling fat man with big ears . . .'

Getting into the role involved some research and a little stretching of the imagination for Keanu. 'I started to meditate and read about Buddhism,' he said of his preparations to film in Nepal with Bertolucci. 'I started to think about old age, suffering and death. You really try to have an emotive experience with the suffering of other sentient beings. That's a beginning. I packed one suitcase – most of it was books – and I just went. The falling away of accoutrements was easy.'

Director Bertolucci came up with a notion which for Keanu was the key to playing the part. 'About 30 hours before I was due to utter my first words, Bernardo said "I think Siddhartha should have some kinda accent." He works very instinctually and in the moment, which I love, and I think it was a great insight, and the way to go. The accent that I've developed, it's a kinda English-Indian-American . . . Those are the ingredients.'

Sacrifices were the name of the game for Keanu as he had to get in shape for a part that required him to wear little more than a loin cloth. Despite his own preferences for Coke, burgers and beer, Keanu was forced to fast prior to shooting *Little Buddha*. Although Bertolucci had suggested having a stand-in for the star for the scenes of Siddhartha's six-year fast, Keanu was having none of it and proceeded to shed the pounds himself. It led to some interesting nightmares when on location. 'I dreamed about bread and cheese,' he said of his fasting nightmare, 'and pouring wine on my head while I rolled naked in the dirt . . .'

His diet was, however, worthwhile when he got to Kathmandu, as an inspection

On the verge of turning 30, Keanu finally moved beyond the high school teen roles that continued to haunt him due to his youthful looks.

by local Buddhists passed him for the role. 'I remember I was in my underwear parading back and forth in front of monks and lamas, and all the monks are looking at my feet and my hands, checking me out. It was like being inspected by the police. They'd say things like, "Yes, we asked the Oracle and it is good you are playing this part."'

Having passed the inspection, Keanu was soon deep in the role he'd come to play, adopting Buddhist beliefs, some of which even stayed with him for a while after returning to the United States. 'When I came home I felt really different,' he confessed. 'It was surreal, you know, the bombarding pace here in LA. I never took refuge, though. I realised that in order to continue to be an actor, I couldn't do that. I don't come from a tradition of meditation. I've kind of opened a new book and through that, it's become relevant. There's certainly that attraction to go over the hill and become a yogi...'

'I was very happy to be in Kathmandu,' he recalled. 'It was incredible, the cows in the road...' There were things, particularly the increasing tourism, which didn't sit so well with the actor. 'Through these 900-year-old cities with cows and children and houses that barely have electricity come, you know, Mercedes-Benz tourist buses with windows that don't even open, full of a hundred tourists totally enclosed in their environment, which I guess is good, as opposed to a hundred people marching through some village. There seems to be no happy medium.'

There were very physical problems for Keanu and the whole *Little Buddha* production team during their stay in Nepal. 'Coming to Kathmandu, you realise why America is so clean,' said the star. 'There's shit everywhere in those medieval villages. I'm sure when the Americans colonised they must have just wanted to get that out of their paths, outta the sewers, just get it clean.' The local sanitary conditions were to result in an outbreak of diarrhoea, an affliction which Keanu's star status did not

Jeremy Thomas and Bernardo Bertolucci with Keanu.

prevent him from experiencing. 'Oh, yeah. I was at a monastery. As I was eating the rice and potatoes, I was told by a local Nepalese, "Oh, yes – Europeans come and eat here sometimes and they get very sick. Europeans and their weak stomachs." There I was with a fever and the shits, having to do the Lotus – Hold. . .it. . .in. . .'

Filming on the project brought Keanu's *Bill and Ted* surfer dude persona up against some rather different kinds of belief. In particular, Keanu worked with Khyentse Rinpoche, a revered local dignitary. 'He was this man that helped Bertolucci,' recalled Keanu. 'He's venerable. We'd go to this town and the leader of the army would prostrate to this man. And I'm going, "Hey, man, how's it going?"' Keanu even took to indulging in evening strolls around the area of filming, wearing Buddhist robes and huge boots, greeting children and even female fans who'd seen him in the video release of *Point Break*.

Keanu was impressed with Bertolucci's control over the circus that filming *Little Buddha* in Nepal inevitably became. 'He had elephants who were walking off the set, 500 extras who couldn't get in their costumes, the sun was coming up, they didn't have fog, the horse was stepping on people! It was totally crazy, like the horse didn't like the elephants, it was insane, but Bertolucci was, like, kind of hanging out. He was very intense about having it happen.'

Hoping a little of the magic of Bertolucci's *The Last Emperor* would rub off on this film and perhaps on himself, Keanu was keen on the visual impact *Little Buddha* might make. 'Bernardo doesn't storyboard. A lot of storyboarding is done so that producers have an idea of what the director is looking at. Bernardo has this vision and he comes to a place and he responds organically and he comes up with something. You're working with a master, so it's a more complex process than Hollywood, but sometimes it's outrageously simple.'

When it was all over, Keanu thought the film had come out well, considering the topics being dealt with. 'I thought the film was very poetic . . . about the whole aspect of prophets, karma and reincarnation . . . your place in all of that . . . [it's] complicated.'

For *Little Buddha* producer Jeremy Thomas, who is also chairman of the British Film Institute, there was something inscrutable about Keanu and his performance. 'Keanu is exotic. He has a look that could be translated into Siddhartha, but I can't really tell you too much about him, except that I enjoyed working with him and would like to again. I think he's a maturing actor, and he's going to do some beautiful work in the future. He chooses his work and he's a self-contained person.'

Thomas thought Keanu had succeeded in what was in certain respects a 'dangerous role', while Bertolucci himself was more than pleased with the overall outcome of his film. 'I thought so much about this problem,' he said of his attempt to capture the essence of Siddhartha in Keanu's performance. 'I think this is the first time I have a kind of happy ending in one of my films. I always thought a happy ending was Hollywood nonsense, but here it is a very natural thing.'

Reaction to Keanu's turn in *Little Buddha* was mixed – definitely an improvement on the universal condemnation his Jonathan Harker had received in *Bram Stoker's Dracula*. For Richard Shickel, writing in *Time* magazine, Keanu had surprisingly pulled off something of an acting coup: 'Siddhartha is played with improbable persuasiveness by Keanu Reeves, another of Bertolucci's eccentric choices in *Little Buddha* that pays off.' For *Variety*, he was a 'surprisingly watchable and dashing Siddhartha'.

As with some of Keanu's previous films, his performance was more criticised in the British press, where reviewers took a somewhat cynical approach to

Keanu's trip to Nepal for Little Buddha *gave the actor time for a period of reflection on his life.*

Keanu with Sofia Coppola, one of several women the actor has been linked with.

Bertolucci's efforts to make Buddhism accessible in a family-oriented film. Writing in *Empire* magazine, critic Kim Newman wrote: 'Keanu's Peter Sellers-esque Indian accent isn't much help and his Nautilus physique looks nothing like all the older Buddha you've ever seen.'

Some British critics found themselves impressed by Keanu's portrayal, however. Geoff Brown in *The Times*, for example, was pleasantly surprised: 'Given his gauche performances in past period roles, Keanu's portrayal of young Siddhartha is surprisingly persuasive.'

Released first in Italy and Germany, Bertolucci withdrew *Little Buddha* in order to re-edit the film for the American market, losing about eighteen minutes. It was in vain, though, as the film sadly sank without trace, having only a modest afterlife on video. Neither the art-house cachet of Bertolucci nor the teen appeal of Keanu Reeves was enough to rescue the film from box office failure. Although visually stunning, its curious mix of pure storytelling and elaborate exoticism was often interpreted as simple-minded kitsch.

Little Buddha had proved a worthwhile exercise for Keanu Reeves. On the verge of turning 30, the actor was finally realising his ambition to move beyond the teen high-schooler roles that had kick-started his career and continued to haunt him due to his youthful looks. 'The innocence certainly comes across in the performance. I'm certainly not playing the commander of the army or a father of eight. But in general I don't want to be in high school or losing my virginity anymore. . .'

However different the part in *Little Buddha* was, it still had broad thematic similarities with other roles Keanu had played, and indeed was a good fit for his own public persona. 'The only consistency I can see in my work upon reflection is that there's always been an innocence to my characterisations,' admitted Keanu. 'That's changing, but I'm still innocent because I'm an idiot. Which is, you know, a drag . . .'

Still without any prominent romantic life, Keanu had become linked with several women during the period. Long before the marriage of Kenneth Branagh and Emma Thompson had officially broken up, Keanu was cited as having enjoyed a liaison with the actress during the filming of *Much Ado About Nothing*, although he had expressed more interest in Kate Beckinsale, who played Hero. It was an interest that was not reciprocated by the young actress. Thompson had fuelled the rumours by referring to Keanu during an awards ceremony speech where she thanked him for 'undressing in front of me'.

During this time Keanu was also said to have been involved with Sofia Coppola, daughter of *Bram Stoker's Dracula* director Francis Ford Coppola. She had replaced Winona Ryder at the last minute on her father's *The Godfather Part III*, and had been heavily criticised for her performance. Keanu had met and hit it off with her during the shooting of *Dracula*, and the pair saw each other on and off for some time afterwards. But still, there was no long-lasting relationship for Keanu.

As he approached 30, Keanu Reeves knew that a more mature approach to his roles was required. He'd finally escaped the teen parts, but the innocent aura that surrounded him as a person meant that he still received the call when a part like *Little Buddha* or Jonathan Harker came up. 'The opportunity for maturity is definitely there,' he admitted when considering his next move. 'I'm very interested in becoming a better actor, but I'm still kind of floating along.' There was, however, a role on the horizon awaiting Keanu that would mean his coasting days were over.

CHAPTER SEVEN

Speeding to Success

T HE YEAR 1994 was to be a pivotal one for Keanu Reeves. Without a
substantial hit since 1992's Bram Stoker's *Dracula*, Keanu's star had waned
somewhat in Hollywood. He'd been indulgent in his film choices, having fun
with his pal Alex Winter in *Freaked* and playing Don John in Kenneth Branagh's
Much Ado About Nothing. 'Much ado about nothing' was exactly what critics began to
think about Keanu's lauded career and pin-up status. Once again, he was in the
position of being considered one of cinema's prime heart-throbs, without actually
having recently played a part on screen that would have cemented that iconic role.
Nonetheless, he'd been working with top name and experimental directors alike:
Bernardo Bertolucci and Gus Van Sant on *Little Buddha* and *Even Cowgirls Get the
Blues* alone.

Things were to change with Jan De Bont's *Speed*. Finally, Keanu Reeves was to
play a straightforward, action hero role in a slam-bam, summer box office
blockbuster. It seemed for Keanu as though the fan adoration had come first, only
later to be followed by the career-making film.

Speed was to be dubbed '*Die Hard* on a bus', and the plot was simple enough to
be encapsulated in that high concept phrase. Dennis Hopper plays an ex-cop out
for revenge who taunts Keanu's high-flying bomb disposal expert Jack Traven.
Wiring up a Los Angeles city bus to explode if it slows down below fifty miles an
hour, Keanu's cop teams up with bus passenger Annie (Sandra Bullock) to keep the
vehicle on the road and out of danger. De Bont saw the appeal of the film as being
'regular people on a regular bus doing something highly irregular'.

De Bont was looking for a new type of action hero, a younger, more sensitive
and vulnerable action man. 'A lot more like a real person,' was De Bont's
description of the *Speed* script's central character of Jack Traven, 'and not looking
giant and muscular all the time.'

The casting of Keanu Reeves as this new, sensitive action hero should not have
been the surprise that many saw it as. After all, he'd almost rehearsed the role in
Kathryn Bigelow's surf-cop movie *Point Break* several years ago. De Bont had seen
that movie and thought Keanu's turn as the FBI agent was perfect for *Speed*. 'I'd
seen scenes in it where I'd gone "Oh, my God, if he grows up a little bit, he might
be really good."'

Although De Bont was enamoured of the *Speed* script the same couldn't be said
for Keanu's initial reaction. After all, being an action icon was not high on the

Keanu rehearsing with Speed *director Jan De Bont.*

actor's agenda. He was worried that his character of Jack Traven was too much in the *Die Hard* mould, dropping too many Bruce Willis-style one-liners, but he was captivated by the overall premise of the film. 'The bus and the bomb, fantastically fantastic,' he enthused. 'It was so silly, I felt it could bomb, but with the right guy . . . and Jan, he had a – I guess the word is vision – he knew what he wanted to do, and it actually seemed like it would be fun. I don't mean to use such a coy term, but he had an enthusiasm for it. He seemed like a man with a mission.'

Although Keanu was cool at first towards the prospect of starring in a summer action movie, his advisers agreed it would do the star's career no harm whatsoever and might in fact do him a lot of good.

With revisions underway on the script, worries began to emanate from the studio – 20th Century Fox – about the cast De Bont had assembled. Unconvinced of Keanu's potential as an action hero, studio bosses wanted him teamed up with a big-name actress in the heroine role as a box office insurance policy.

'Because they think he's not a star yet, they said if we take him we have to get a famous actress next to him, so at least audiences have something to build on,' admitted De Bont. 'I told them, "You cannot look at it that way." You have to find the perfect combination. I want someone who is going to drive a bus who you can believe in, not a beautiful face, but a strong feisty woman.'

In the end De Bont got both in the shape of Sandra Bullock, then relatively unknown, having appeared in low budget films like *Love Potion No. 9* and opposite Sylvester Stallone in *Demolition Man*. 'Fox didn't want to go with it for a long time,' lamented De Bont, 'and only two weeks, or less, before shooting they agreed to go with her. It was like a nightmare, but they are a good combination.'

In the finished film, Bullock and Keanu come across well on screen, but they also developed a strong rapport during shooting, with the established star willing to go the extra mile to help the performance of the newcomer. 'He was so great to work with,' said Bullock. 'He didn't have to be there at five o'clock in the morning for my reversal shot, but he walked out of his trailer and said, "I just waited because I knew you needed me for that scene." And that's rare. People go crazy over him, and they have every reason to, because he's good-looking on the inside, too.'

So strong was the association between Keanu and Bullock that crew members on *Speed* speculated that the two were having an affair. 'He's a kind, beautiful person,' said Bullock of Keanu, speaking of her co-star in the most glowing terms. 'There are so many beautiful people in this world, and that's not what gets me. That's a dime a dozen and it gets old. Then you meet somebody who happens to be blessed that way and is one of the kindest, most respectful people that'll you'll ever meet and that's Keanu.' It was her leading man's sense of humour which struck a chord with Bullock. 'You know, Keanu's an incredibly funny guy, and he doesn't think he is. The first thing he ever said to me was "I don't have a sense of humour." Progressively, I think

Star turns: both Sandra Bullock and Keanu emerged from Speed *as big Hollywood stars.*

Keanu's new, very short haircut worried studio executives who thought he should wear a wig in Speed.

we discovered it. He was courteous and kind and void of any ego. He's like a cat.'

Bullock was even more pleased that Keanu wasn't an all-macho action hero in the style of Stallone or Schwarzenegger. 'I liked it that Keanu wasn't always the capable male, he couldn't always keep it together, and depended on a woman just as strong as he was. It didn't make him less masculine. It just made him human.'

Whether Keanu and Sandra Bullock were ever more than just good friends during the filming of *Speed* remains a mystery. As so often in the past, Keanu contrived to keep his private life out of the pages of the tabloids by simply appearing not to have one.

With his cast finally in place and his new script approved, De Bont was ready to roll the cameras on *Speed*. There was one final hold up, however, which almost scuppered the entire project – Keanu's dramatic new haircut.

De Bont had insisted on a severe haircut for his leading man. 'I had what they call a one cut,' joked Keanu, 'and then I took the "one" off on the clippers! Some people thought it was too extreme because they could see my scalp.'

The studio executives were prime among them, insisting to De Bont that a wig be obtained for Keanu pronto. 'They saw him walking on the lot and they called me right away. They said, "Who told him to cut his hair? We have to get him a wig – now!" I said, "No way are we going to get him a wig." They called his manager, they called his agent, they said, "We're going to have to postpone this movie now," and I said, "No, we have two more weeks, and in two weeks his hair will grow this much. It's great, it's what I want." They were totally upset.'

Another aspect of Keanu's appearance had to be tinkered with: his physique. 'The thing with Keanu,' said De Bont, 'is that he looks very boyish and I wanted him to be like a young adult. I didn't want him to be like a kid – and he loves to be like a kid.' De Bont had Keanu pump up just a little, trying to keep his physique the right side of believability.

Filming finally got underway in late summer 1993. To try to get him into the spirit of the film, De Bont suggested that Keanu might like to try his hand – and some other important body parts – at doing his own stunts. 'I said, "You drive the Jaguar during the scenes swerving through the cars . . ." And when he did he started to like it so much, he said: "Action movies can be fun." He got some kind of adrenalin rush, from that moment on, every day. He was there all the time, and whenever possible he wanted to do it all himself, because it is exciting. That's the young character in him who wants to experience everything himself first-hand.'

Keanu ended up doing about 90 per cent of the stunt work in *Speed* himself, adding to the believability of the film and to the action icon image of the actor that emerged more clearly upon the film's worldwide release. 'I got to be pretty involved,' admitted Keanu, after his initially reluctant stance towards the film. 'It was one of the lessons I learned from *Point Break* : that the more you can have me in there, the better it is. Gary Himes, the stunt co-ordinator, and Jan were very good about setting up situations that looked like I was in peril and let me get in there and do it.

'I surprised myself,' admitted Keanu. 'It was great to participate and get as close as I could. I enjoy that sort of pressure and excitement very much.' Not all the action moments were the real Keanu, however. He's too valuable a property for that. 'That last scene of someone going under the bus is a stuntman. I didn't do really tough stunts, other people get paid to do that sort of life-threatening thing.'

With good progress being made on the film, an unexpected hiatus occurred for Keanu Reeves at the end of October 1993, caused by the death of his friend and occasional co-star River Phoenix. Phoenix died of a drug overdose on the sidewalk of Sunset Strip outside the Viper Room, a trendy night-spot owned by another teen heart-throb actor, Johnny Depp.

Keanu was deeply affected by the death of Phoenix, and so Jan De Bont rejigged his tough filming schedule to cut the grieving actor a little slack. 'It was a terrible shock,' said Keanu of the death of his friend, after refusing to comment on the incident for a long time. 'I miss him very much. I think of it as an accident . . . I can't make any sense of it.'

Switching around the schedule on *Speed*, De Bont made sure that Keanu had some less demanding scenes to work on while he came to terms with the loss of his friend. 'He took it very hard,' recalled the director. 'He became very quiet. It took him a while to calm down. . .it scared the hell out of him.'

Keanu did come to terms with the death of River Phoenix, and was able to see what he had gained from knowing Phoenix. 'River was a really heavy actor . . . he was the best. It helped me a lot to work with him. He was really inspiring and intelligent. All I can say is I've never felt a thing like that before in my life. I was very sad, and something beyond sad. I don't know what it is, just that you sob for hours. . .'

'Get ready for rush hour' was the inspired marketing slogan used to promote

Speed upon its June 1994 American release. With spectacularly good reviews and excellent word-of-mouth about what a rush the film was, *Speed* reached an American box office gross of over $100 million in just seven weeks.

Split into three distinct sections, *Speed* has Keanu's Jack Traven dealing with a plummeting lift in the opening sequence, the bomb on the bus that will explode if the speed falls below 50mph, and a final, out-of-control train on the under-construction LA subway. Each situation is almost enough on its own for a whole movie, but the three together give *Speed* its headlong energetic drive. De Bont's direction and the script by Yost and Wheedon reduced the action film to its bare essentials – a series of blockbusting action sequences with nothing in between. There's no character development – Keanu is the hero, Hopper is the bomb-making nutter, Jeff Daniels is the buddy who gets sacrificed to the villain's plans, and Sandra Bullock – in her star-making performance – is the ordinary gal thrust into an extraordinary situation. There's no real plot, either, just a series of events for the hero to deal with. While all these aspects might be negative in most other films, here they all contribute to the out-and-out success of *Speed*, one of the first films to bring the theme-park-ride-type experience directly into movies.

Writing in *Time* magazine, Richard Schickel saw that *Speed*'s 'sheer cut-to-the chase straightforwardness is part of its appeal. . . It is executed with panache and utter conviction.' *Empire* enthused that *Speed* was a 'fabulous trip. . . As for Keanu Reeves, the ongoing debate of his so-called acting skills is finally put to rest here (clue: he can't) by virtue of his sheer star power and sex appeal, gradually stripping down as the movie progresses and turning himself into the '90s leading man in the process. An addictive blast of pure adrenalin. . .the knee-tremblin' white-knuckle ride of the year.'

Keanu had become, as a result of *Speed*, a cultural icon in his own right. In the *Sunday Times*, writer and cultural critic Julie Burchill penned a devastating analysis

Keanu tangles with Dennis Hopper in Speed. *The pair had previously worked together in* River's Edge.

A new action icon: Keanu aimed to be a more believable hero in Speed.

of Keanu's career to date. 'Brigitte, Marilyn, Winona, Raquel, and now Keanu. Like Bardot, he rarely speaks in English in his films, and his attempts to do so are charming to behold. And as with her, it is highly unlikely that his beauty will ever allow him to be dispassionately rated as an actor.'

It was not so bizarre a comparison as it might have seemed at first, as Keanu Reeves did share more in common with the great screen goddesses, like Marilyn Monroe or Brigitte Bardot, than he does with great screen actors. He has been defined through his career by his looks, and his acting ability always came secondary to his star power, a power intimately wrapped up with his sculpted cheek bones, Chinese-Hawaiian, almost Asian looks. In his films he is the sexually passive character, having things happen around him rather than functioning as the driving force behind the action. In his films he is a loser at the game of romance, just as he seemed to have difficulties with relationships in real life. In *Bram Stoker's Dracula,* his wife-to-be Winona Ryder fell for Gary Oldman, while in *Dangerous Liaisons* Uma Thurman preferred John Malkovich. For an actor whose very appeal was so wrapped up with sex, it seems amazing that there should be so little sex in his films and in his life. In *Speed,* hero and heroine get no further down the road to romance than a passionate clinch on the ground at the climax. Sexually, Keanu

Keanu and Sandra Bullock enjoy a passionate clinch on the ground at the climax of Speed.

Reeves is an enigma. For a young cinematic sex symbol, the irony was that Keanu has played very few romantic roles.

At the height of his success with *Speed*, Keanu Reeves had to confront a question that had been hanging around his neck for years in Hollywood, but was rarely referred to openly: was he gay?

Rarely seen out on the town with female companionship and hardly ever written about in the tabloids in terms of dating the latest Hollywood starlet, Keanu avoided the kind of press coverage the likes of Johnny Depp and Brad Pitt had attracted to their love lives.

The issue was thrown into sharp relief when a rumour about Keanu spread around the world like wildfire: the actor had supposedly secretly 'married' media mogul David Geffen in a beach-front ceremony in Mexico, followed by a $15,000 spending spree on Geffen's charge card. The story seemed to have first been published in Italian and Spanish newspapers before winding its way back to Los Angeles and New York.

Stories that Keanu Reeves might be gay dated back at least five years when he played around during a session for *Interview* magazine. Asked outright if he was gay, Keanu denied it, but then, mischievously, added, 'But ya never know. . .' It was an answer that recalled his days on the Toronto stage in *Wolfboy*, the controversial gay-themed play that had kick-started his acting career and so cheered Toronto's gay community.

His performance alongside River Phoenix in Gus Van Sant's gay rent-boy drama *My Own Private Idaho* had done nothing to dampen the speculation. River Phoenix was more comfortable with gossip about his sexuality – including supposed liaisons with R.E.M.'s Michael Stipe and an unnamed British actor – than Keanu Reeves was ever to be.

His lack of high profile romances in the intervening years had only served to give the rumours some credence. In the absence of any definite information, the void was filled with speculation, unsubstantiated stories and downright untrue reports of Keanu's activities. Keanu always attributed his lack of high profile female companionship to the demands of his professional life. 'The thing is, the kind of person I am depends on the day. The biggest sacrifice I've made is the chance of success in love. [The worst thing about being famous is] losing out on love. . .'

It wasn't until the David Geffen tale became widespread public knowledge that Keanu Reeves was forced to tackle the subject head on again. Geffen, a film producer and record label mogul, is now part of the triumvirate (with Steven Spielberg and Jeffrey Katzenberger) behind the new super studio Dreamworks SKG. Upfront about his homosexuality, he never expected to be romantically connected with Keanu Reeves. 'I've never laid eyes on him,' protested Geffen. 'It's a phenomenon: people make this stuff up. I even had a friend say that his trainer was at the wedding. You think I could keep something like that secret? And then people saying I bought Keanu $15,000 worth of clothes at Barney's? I mean, come on. I'd buy him some clothes, but he doesn't need that. It's just an ugly, mean-spirited rumour, meant to hurt him because he's a movie star.'

For his part, Keanu maintained a well-balanced reaction to the bizarre tale. 'It's so ridiculous, I find it funny. I mean, there's nothing wrong with being gay, so to deny it is to make a judgement. Why make a big deal of it? If someone doesn't want to hire me because they think I'm gay, well, then I have to deal with it, I guess. Or if people were picketing a theatre, but otherwise, it's just gossip, isn't it.'

Gossip it may have been, but Keanu's handlers and managers organised an all-out PR campaign to set the record straight, even allowing the star to give a lengthy interview to American gay magazine *Out*. 'My manager and agent said I had to address it, because it was getting in the way of work and just freaking people out, so I said "Okay",' said Keanu of agreeing to the magazine piece. 'Otherwise, I wouldn't have. I just took the advice of people whom I've hired for professional aspects.'

Keanu opened the *Out* piece by proclaiming: 'I don't really talk about my private life and I guess my public life is pretty boring.' It didn't take long for the interview to get around to the subject of David Geffen. 'I first heard it when I was in Winnipeg [for *Hamlet*], on my answering machine. My friend Claire called. She said, "I heard you got married, congratulations." I didn't really think much about it. I guess I have to say I've never met the guy.'

At the time, Keanu approached this breach in his public image calmly and quietly, following his managers' crisis management instructions, but the rumours, innuendoes and untrue stories revealed to Keanu the downside of his kind of public life. He'd always sought to shield his private life, seeing it as a separate realm from his public persona. That very process, however, had given rise to

Gay or straight, Keanu's elusive romantic life attracted the attention of the paparazzi.

bizarre unfounded speculation that could potentially have done more harm than the rather unexciting truth. However, part of his appeal was undoubtedly down to this sexual ambiguity.

'It's nobody's business,' Keanu later angrily said, reacting to constant press enquiries about his off-screen affairs. 'I fucking hate it, it's a drag. It's very funny, though. Especially in America, there's this thinking that "you're a public figure, so I'm allowed to ask you anything". I wouldn't mind so much if it was somehow related to the creative act, as opposed to just trying to get gossip or trying to get to know me.'

For all their efforts, neither Keanu nor David Geffen was able to totally kill the story. The idea of a beach-front New Age marriage ceremony between the two proved too compelling – even if it wasn't true – and further elaborations on the tale continued to appear. According to reports in the *Toronto Star*, Geffen was a frequent visitor to see Keanu play *Hamlet*, while at the same time other reports had

Keanu dating a male dancer from the Royal Winnipeg Ballet.

The aftermath of the Geffen affair was one of the few times when Keanu allowed his carefully constructed, airhead-inspired public interview persona to slip, showing clearly a glimpse of the intelligent man beneath, who is more savvy than many give him credit for. 'I still have people asking me about River [Phoenix] in an interview where they have three minutes. It's like "tell me how you felt", and I'm astounded, because they want to have a moment of seeing whether a person's affected or not.'

Such was the fallout that Keanu resolved not to read his own press any more. 'No, I don't read anything any more. I'm too angry. I'm tired of being misrepresented, misquoted, manipulated, being put on a pedestal, being knocked down – it's all just too much trouble. I have to admit to feeling like the critics' whipping boy. You know what, it used to bug me, but now, being a Virgo, digging the masochism, I kind of like it. I think it's funny.'

Keanu Reeves easily recovered from the David Geffen episode, and all people remembered from 1994 was the success of *Speed*, which, naturally, did him no harm whatsoever. The most immediate effect was a 600 per cent increase in his salary, with film offers now coming in at $7 million a throw. With *Speed*, Keanu firmly joined the A-list of Hollywood stars as well as that special breed of all-out action hero. He'd played the Hollywood game their way, for a change, and he'd still come out on top.

Keanu Reeves refused, however, to take the obvious route into action hero bankability after *Speed*. Once was enough for the time being. Keanu felt a need to return to the stage after his bus and bomb heroics, and the part of Hamlet was a role he'd harboured a long-standing ambition to play. In addition, he signed up to play the lead in the film *Johnny Mnemonic*. Before this, though, Keanu had a family problem to deal with.

CHAPTER EIGHT

Head in the Clouds

A T THE TIME of his greatest triumph on screen in *Speed*, and having managed to shake off the ludicrous rumours connecting him romantically with David Geffen, further trouble hit Keanu Reeves. His father, Samuel, whom Keanu had not seen since his teenage years, was arrested in a blaze of publicity at Hilo airport in Hawaii. The charges related to serious drug-trafficking offences, as Samuel had been caught in possession of large amounts of cocaine and heroin, and was accused of having dealings with a major Mexican drug-smuggling gang.

Police had been on Samuel's trail for weeks, keeping close watch on the rotund middle-aged man and his farmhouse in Hilo. Based on a tip-off from a neighbour, the undercover cops followed Samuel and a companion to the local airport where they finally pounced, grabbing the pair with a consignment of heroin and cocaine.

Arrested with Samuel was Hermilo Castillo, 24, said to be a member of a Mexican crime family. Castillo promptly put up $100,000 bail and immediately skipped the country, leaving Keanu's father alone to face the music for smuggling 'black tar' heroin onto the island.

Appearing in court on 21 June 1994, Samuel Nowlin Reeves accepted his guilt on a reduced charge of 'promoting a dangerous drug in the second degree'. His arguments that drugs should be legalised and that he was doing no harm, combined with his past record relating to drugs, had served to curse Samuel Reeves. A ten-year sentence in Halawa State Prison, near Pearl Harbor, was the result.

Although he was estranged from his long-absent father, it was clear to Keanu that he could not escape the fall-out from his father's jailing, even if he wished to pretend otherwise. 'I don't want to talk about him,' was the standard response from Keanu to press questions. 'He disappeared out of my life when I was a kid.'

Despite his evasion and his determination to avoid talking about his father, it was clear that Samuel had been a major influence on the life of Keanu, largely through his absence. 'I think a lot of who I am is a reaction against his action. [As a father] I would, first of all, try to be around.' Shy and lonely as a child, Keanu had never recovered from his abandonment by his father at the age of thirteen. Despite his superstardom, thoughts of his father could easily push Keanu back to the feelings that dominated his teenage years – and now at the height of his success, his father had come back to haunt him with a vengeance.

Although Keanu kept quiet about his father's arrest, his cousin, Leslie Reeves, was happy to speak out on the star's behalf. 'When he heard his father had been arrested, Keanu was angry. He said, "Who the hell needs this?" He does not love his father. He has nothing but contempt for him. He hates him.' Added Keanu's childhood pal, Shawn Aberle, 'He really resented the way he felt his father had abandoned him.'

Yet it was that abandonment that drove Keanu to show he could do better than his father before him, and despite his fortune and the fact that he lived and worked amid countless temptations in Hollywood, he was determined to avoid the traps of drug addiction. He had seen how that lifestyle had ended up for both his actor friend River Phoenix and for his now jailed father. They were mistakes Keanu Reeves was determined to learn from.

The original source material for the film *Johnny Mnemonic* was a short story by renowned 'cyberpunk' author William Gibson. Gibson coined the concept of 'cyberspace' in the early 1980s ('They'll never let me forget it'), long before the Internet became the phenomenon it is today. Although he started writing science fiction in 1977, Gibson is still best known for his trilogy of *Neuromancer, Count Zero* and *Mona Lisa Overdrive*, published between 1981 and 1988. *Neuromancer* brought Gibson the Hugo, Nebula and Philip K. Dick awards, as well as acres of mainstream press coverage.

Originally, *Johnny Mnemonic* was set up under the auspices of Carolco Pictures, but due to financial difficulties the property was put into 'turnaround', meaning it

Ice T, Keanu and Dina Meyer in Johnny Mnemonic.

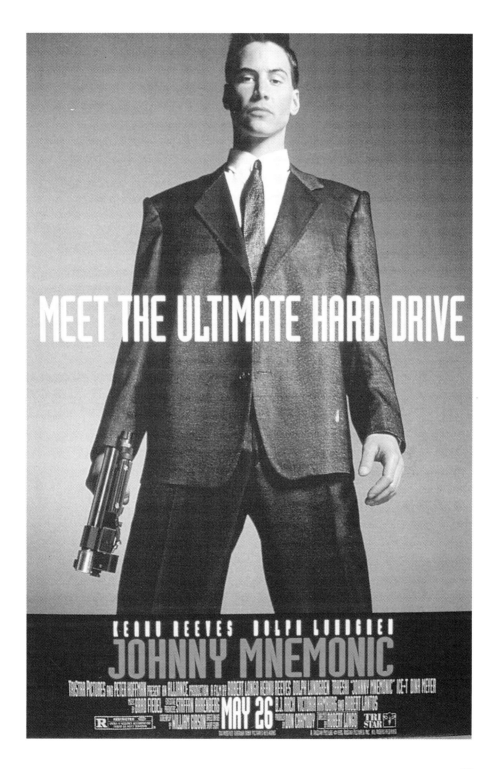

was available to be picked up by another studio or producer once they'd paid off Carolco's development costs to date.

The project was picked up by an ex-Carolco producer and Gibson fan Peter Hoffman, who hired *Terminator 2: Judgement Day* and *Total Recall* producer B. J. Rack to 'midwife' the project into existence. The proposed director was artist Robert Longo, a fixture of the New York avant garde art world. In the so-hip-it-hurt cast were post-punk performer Henry Rollins, rapper Ice T and Japanese cult figure 'Beat' Takeshi Kitano.

Before Keanu Reeves landed the part, Val Kilmer was originally signed to the title role of *Johnny Mnemonic*. 'I had some conversations with him about the role,' said Gibson of Kilmer. 'Then I woke up one day and, lo and behold, he wasn't in it. I think Val could have done a very dramatic job, but it would have been different. That's the strange thing with casting, it can really change a movie.' Kilmer's PR people told *Premiere* magazine: 'Val did everything possible to resolve creative and financial differences, but they never were, so he left.'

The intrigue of the cast change extended to how the script found its way to Keanu Reeves. The actor didn't get the script through his agency Creative Artists Agency (CAA), which also represented Kilmer and may have recognised a conflict of interests. 'It arrived on my doorstep,' insisted Keanu. 'It was given to me by a friend of a friend. When I saw William Gibson's name on the credits, I was like, "Cool." I had read *Neuromancer* when it came out, and I was a great fan of it. I said, "Yeah, I'd like to work on this."'

In fact, the script was sent to Keanu through a drive-by delivery, tossed into his yard from a passing car. Keanu was not a sure-fire action star, as he was in production on *Speed* at the time, so TriStar executive Chris Lee had a tough time convincing the studio that he was the right guy for the part. Keanu was also going to be a more expensive option than Kilmer, his asking price being in the region of $1 to $1.5 million per film before the release of *Speed*, resulting in TriStar putting up the additional money in exchange for the video distribution rights to the finished film.

The casting of Keanu Reeves was the final element that allowed Gibson to bring his title character fully into focus. 'In the beginning he's a slick, superficial, robotic asshole. As he bumps into more and more terrible immovable objects, the surface starts to crack, and underneath is this vulnerable human being. Keanu gave me real crucial help in figuring out this character, because people were always saying, "We don't get the motivation on this guy." Keanu asked me early on where this guy was coming from and what's he really like, and I'm like, "I don't know." That was the beginning of his interpretation of the character. It was utterly crucial that he developed those wonderfully subtle, robotic twitches and ways of moving.'

Keanu was only too aware of the casting musical chairs and the actor had concerns about the script, which he talked over with Gibson and Longo. 'The film in its final incarnation is so different from where it began,' he admitted. 'I play the title character who has the capacity to store computer data in his head. In order to have that capacity, I've had my long-term memory, mostly dealing with my childhood, removed. My character didn't care that he'd had his memory erased.'

Keanu felt this disinterest in the character's background was a mistake, and his concerns resulted in Gibson and Longo altering the dynamics of the *Johnny Mnemonic* script. 'They decided to make it so that he does care, so the whole journey of this hero is to regain his childhood.'

The plot of *Johnny Mnemonic* has Johnny transporting some valuable information in his head. But now, Johnny wants out and he goes on the run with the information and his female bodyguard. In pursuit are various parties all interested on getting their hand on the data in his head. Additionally, he must download the information within a set time scale, otherwise his brain will overload and go pop! Journeying through a nightmarish technological future, the mismatched pair find themselves in 'heaven', a low tech hide-out for society's technological underclass.

Tackling the multi-faceted role was something of a challenge for Keanu, after the straightforward heroics and running and jumping of *Speed*. 'I was really dealing with an unconscious anger for this character,' he said. 'There was a level where I worked with Robert [Longo] on the angularity of the character. He was hard-edged. He's not the nicest guy in the world. His job demanded a kind of aggressiveness, in terms of controlling a room and making sure of his safety. When I get uploaded with the data, I'm at such a disadvantage. I'm unaware of everything around me, and it's kind of a shady business that I work in.'

Coming off *Speed*, taking on the relatively low budget production of *Johnny Mnemonic* was a different experience for Keanu. 'I call it a big budget, low budget picture. We didn't have a long shooting schedule so that put quite a demanding pace to the filming, which I dug. It had its good and bad aspects. It makes you pare down and be aggressive in a different way, but sometimes it does induce more compromise. Robert had some quite unique cinematic ambitions which were not allowed to be explored because we didn't have the time or the money to do that.

With a novice director – a painter no less – handling a $30 million film, with a script from a heavily involved writer who had no real movie experience and a last minute replacement for the leading actor, *Johnny Mnemonic* was fated to be not without its problems. Many seemed to stem from Robert Longo's inexperience in organising the hundred or so people that make up even a small film crew. According to some on the set, whenever Longo issued an instruction some war-weary members of the crew would whistle the tune 'If Only I Had A Brain' from *The Wizard of Oz*. According to others, Longo was at times overwhelmed by the enormity of the project and so lacked the authority to control the complex production.

Canadian producer Don Carmody, one of the people who rode to the rescue of the film when Val Kilmer left, was detached enough to get to the heart of the problems. 'Robert's a first-time director and he's got a lot of ideas, but he doesn't always know how to implement them. He gets to try things out on me first. If we're running late, I'll pull rank. We have some difficult personalities . . . Keanu can be moody . . .'

Observers on the set of *Johnny Mnemonic* felt Keanu came across as a little reserved, if not downright quiet during the dramatic production process. 'Because of the rigorousness of the shooting schedule and the pace, I really had to conserve my energy. I had just filmed *Speed* and that was very vigorous as well. I was saving my energy for when I had to work. It's not a *Die Hard* or anything in that genre, but there was some running and jumping and dodging bullets. I enjoy that kind of physical work.'

For twelve weeks the cast and crew were located in Toronto and Montreal, shooting on sets constructed to stand in for Beijing, China and Newark, New Jersey, all locations

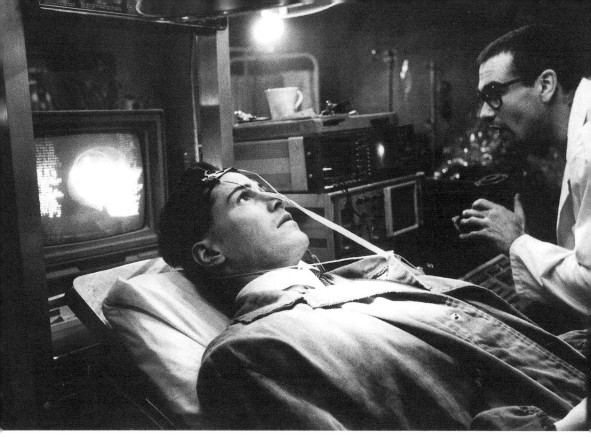

Keanu with Henry Rollins in Johnny Mnemonic: *his character can store computer data in his head.*

in the film's 21st century story. Production designer Nilo Rodis had limited resources to create a future vision to rival that of the 1982 film *Blade Runner* – a future dystopia from Philip K. Dick, realised by director Ridley Scott and often mentioned in the same breath as the ideas of William Gibson. Rodis had to draw on his experience in industrial design and car engineering to come up with the high- and low-tech future of the film.

Gibson, for one, was impressed by Rodis's efforts. 'I realised that for thirteen years I've gone on describing environments like this, and I never expected to see one realised to this degree of resolution. Especially the set for heaven.'

Most critics, however, were not impressed by *Johnny Mnemonic*. For the *Village Voice*, Keanu was 'terrific except when he opens his mouth – and what a great haircut'. The *New York Times* accused Keanu of 'robotic delivery'.

'When my life is over, I'll be remembered for playing Ted,' claimed Keanu once, outlining one of the fears that drove his career after *Speed*. Determined to shake off the airhead image that had shot him to fame once and for all, he didn't want to fall into another trap of playing nothing but action heroes – as he'd just done in *Speed* and *Johnny Mnemonic*. Variety was the spice of his acting life – and he knew his devoted audiences wouldn't necessarily like it.

It wasn't that Keanu was ungrateful for his film success, particularly his new-found fame and wage bracket after *Speed*. He felt capable of much more. 'I did a pretty good job,' he said of *Speed*, 'and it's there on the screen, but I don't really feel like it's my film. I mean, it was great to be in such a successful film, but I don't know how much of that success is down to me. . .'

Keanu continued to be secretive about his off-screen life, denying that he's part of the Hollywood industry or the party scene. 'It gives me a living, but. . .I must admit I've never been very "industry". I don't have enough of a personality. It's true – I lead a very simple and small life. I do go out. I have visited that scene once in a while and I have enjoyed it. I'm always working anyhow.'

When not working on films, though, Keanu professed not to get up to anything special. 'I sit on the couch and indulge whimsies. My current whimsies are coming home, talking to friends and taking voice classes. I do go out once in a while, it's not like I'm a monk.'

This vagueness in Keanu's pronouncements about his off-screen life infuriated his fans, who relied on those who knew him well enough to fill in the many blanks that the star himself left. 'It's interesting,' admitted Gus Van Sant, who'd worked with Keanu twice, 'Keanu's well-read, but he doesn't think he is. And he's very intelligent, but he's a sort of punk rocker, in a way, and he has this façade.'

Part of his façade has been to appear to do nothing with the money he makes. Despite his asking price shooting up to $7 million after *Speed*, he still had no home of his own, with many of his possessions in storage at his sister Kim's home. 'I guess I'm just looking for the right place to live. It's not like I've got this gypsy-bohemian philosophy like, "I don't want a home because I don't want roots."' From hotel to hotel and film to film, Keanu carries with him just one suitcase filled with necessary items. 'I've got it pretty pared down,' he says, claiming only to carry a

Dina Meyer and Keanu in Johnny Mnemonic.

Keanu in A Walk in the Clouds; *his first true romantic lead.*

couple of pairs of trousers, a few T-shirts, socks, underwear, one suit, a sports jacket and a pair of shoes. His only other possessions of any consequences are his two motorcycles and his guitar. So what does he do with all that money, then?

'Ah, what do I do?' responded Keanu to the question in *Vanity Fair*. 'It affords one a certain amount of freedom and travel and I can buy older Bordeaux. I can afford my two Nortons, which is akin to sending a child to a middle-expensive university in the US. But the travel is great.'

Despite his wealth and fame, the biggest concern Keanu has is to project the fact that he's just a normal guy. 'I am normal. Any other kind of perception is a lie, and it just leads to . . . madness. I'm just very grateful to have the opportunity to work, and I'm grateful for people who like it, and so I'm paying respect, as much as I can.'

'I don't want to be super-famous, man,' Keanu said to New York's *Newsday* in 1991. 'That would be awful.' Awful or not, super-famous and a sex symbol is just what he's become following *Speed*. 'I hate that term, "sex symbol". I don't think I'm a sex symbol and I don't think I look like one either.'

His *Johnny Mnemonic* co-star Dina Meyer had definite opinions about Keanu's sex symbol status – and about his inner darkness. 'He thinks he's a nerd! I couldn't believe it. He really thinks he's just some schmo off the street who loves to act. He's very quiet, very introverted,' Meyer told *People* magazine. 'You look at him and can see the wheels turning, but you can't figure him out – if he's happy, if he's sad. . . you just want to say: "What's happening in there?"'

Avoiding talking about his personal life and thoughts was a skill Keanu had cultivated over the years, from first playing the part of Ted in interviews to throw journalists off the scent to later simply restricting his comments to the film he was promoting. 'I think everyone has an inner core they protect – I don't think I'm any different really,' he admitted.

Keanu Reeves went from an action movie double whammy in *Speed* and *Johnny Mnemonic* to his first straight romantic lead in Alfonso Arau's *A Walk in the Clouds*.

Arau had been behind the surprise hit *Like Water for Chocolate*, a steamy tale tinged with a degree of magical realism. His new film told the tale of an American GI returning from war only to become embroiled in a family drama in '40s California. Arau knew he wanted Keanu to play the sensitive GI.

'I said "You can play a very romantic character if you want,"' remembered Arau, feeling that Keanu had the sensitivity for the part, but also had to lose some of his innocence. 'I said, "Keanu, you are going to have to interpret as a grown man, as opposed to an adolescent." You can feel that he has all these emotions below the skin, so I had to open the door for him.'

Based on an Italian film called *Four Steps in the Clouds* and directed by a Mexican film-maker, it tells the story of Paul Sutton (Keanu), a soldier who has had his fair share of hellish experiences. Back home and selling candy on the road, he comes across a distressed woman named Victoria (Aitana Sanchez-Gijon) returning to her family home in the Napa Valley. Dumped by her boyfriend, Victoria is pregnant and unmarried, a scandal in 1945 America. Sensitive shell-shocked soul that he is, Keanu's Paul offers to stand in as her husband to smooth her return home and her relationship with her domineering wine-growing father, played by Anthony Quinn. Of course, the best laid plans can result in the most unexpected outcomes.

A Walk in the Clouds *saw Keanu working with Aitana Sanchez-Gijon and Anthony Quinn.*

Romance in the air: Keanu and Aitana Sanchez-Gijon in A Walk in the Clouds.

For Arau, Keanu was the most suitable actor for this Gary Cooper-inspired ordinary Joe. 'Keanu is like a monk,' he asserted. 'He is devoted to his craft, and has an innocence in his spirit that I liked for this particular character.' Screenwriter Robert Mark Kamen was in full agreement with his director. 'Keanu is incredible. He's romantic, he's sensitive, he's nuanced. It's Keanu like you've never seen him before. . .'

That much at least was true. When Keanu accepted the role in *A Walk in the Clouds*, his action hero debut *Speed* had not yet been released. *Johnny Mnemonic* had not yet bombed. For Keanu, playing an adult romantic lead was something of a radical departure. The nearest he'd come previously was the age-gap comedy-romance of *Aunt Julia and the Scriptwriter*.

'I was shooting *Speed* at the time I met Mr Arau,' explained Keanu of his casting in the role. 'I wanted to do some romance. I was attracted by the passion of the character. There is an honour about him. There is a nice connection between humanity and nature, with the wine and the family and the earth.'

Tackling this romantic character was something of a challenge for the actor. 'The role was a tough test for Keanu,' admitted Arau. 'He was stressed and insecure about it. When I'd ask him to say a romantic phrase differently, I could sense he was worried he'd be criticised. I said, "Trust me, I'm watching over you. . ."'

Keanu recognised the problem within himself. 'There are days when I'm OK,' he said of his approach to acting. 'Maybe it's because I'm a Virgo; it's in my sign to be hard on myself.' Falling back on astrology to explain his difficulties with maintaining a credible performance during a whole film shoot, Keanu again plays up his airhead image. Rather than talk to journalists about the way he constantly strives to act better every time out, Keanu knows that a 'New Age', valley-speak explanation is what's expected from him.

Much was riding on the back of this film for Alfonso Arau. Twentieth Century Fox had entrusted $20 million on Arau's first English-language film on the basis of the success of *Like Water for Chocolate*. 'It's not my calling card to Hollywood,' claimed Arau, 'but to the world market.' No matter how important it may have been, Arau used the stars as his guide. Scheduled to begin shooting on 28 June 1994, Arau moved everything forward a day as his astrologer suggested that the 27th would be a more propitious start date. He may have managed to shoot only one scene on the 27th, but it was enough in his own mind to have met the star-dictated deadline.

'There is a dreamy quality to *Walk*'s set,' said Robert Kamen. That was not only down to the cinematography, but was a product of the fuzzy mind-set that pervaded the key creative personnel on the film. Keanu Reeves was right at home.

That's what some critics felt, too, about Keanu's delve into straight romance. The change of pace from *Speed* was welcomed by most, and *A Walk in the Clouds* went some way to making up for the damage done by the poor performance by *Johnny Mnemonic*. It did good business at the box office and received broadly good reviews. One – the *San Francisco Chronicle* – felt that Keanu had shown himself to be 'a mature, charismatic movie star' and that there was 'not just sweetness there, but depth'. Some critics, however, still had their knives out for Keanu personally, even if audiences seemed happy enough with his screen persona. *People* said: 'Although Keanu is certainly handsome and hunky enough to play the romantic hero, his dogged earnestness and flat-as-a-spatula voice just don't cut it. Combined, these two traits make [him] sound faux-Hemingway and dopey.'

For a change, the British press were more receptive to Keanu in this classic

Keanu on the set of A Walk in the Clouds.

Keanu and Aitana Sanchez-Gijon at the premiere of A Walk in the Clouds.

melodrama. *Empire* magazine simply noted: 'Keanu looks very cute indeed', while the *Guardian* thought he 'pads handsomely through the film'.

After this, Keanu tried his hand at hosting a TV documentary recalling the horrors of the Nazi holocaust. As the host of *Children, Remember the Holocaust* Keanu introduced segments featuring the voices of Kirsten Dunst (*Interview with the Vampire*) and Casey Siemaszko (*Breaking In*). The programme, subtitled *Through Their Eyes*, was part of the award-winning CBS Schoolbreak series of educational documentaries for pre-teens and adolescents. The series explored conflicts facing today's youth and the shows are developed with specialists in education, psychology, religion and related fields.

The one-hour documentary film depicted the Holocaust from the point of view of young people who lived and died under Nazi persecution (1933–1945). One and a half million children and teenagers were killed by Nazis, including Jews, Polish Catholics, Romanies (Gypsies), and the disabled. *Children, Remember the Holocaust* was based on chosen selections from young people's diaries, letters, and survivors' recollections, drawn together by writer D. Shone Kirkpatrick. Using archival film footage, still photography, sound effects, and period music, the film brought the past to life for today's youngsters – who were further attracted to the project by the addition of Keanu Reeves as presenter. In the film the teenage actors speak the thoughts, feelings, dreams, and nightmares that those young people experienced.

Although not Jewish, Keanu had often felt strongly about injustices of all kinds and was happy to lend his name and presence to the project. His community drama school Leah Posluns had been attached to a Jewish community centre, although it was open to all denominations. Keanu's empathy for the Jewish experience seems to have developed from his own sometimes itinerant childhood – and hosting a TV show was not something he'd ever done before. Always game for a new challenge, he threw himself into the project, even though it would prove to be no more than a minor footnote in his screen career.

Children, Remember the Holocaust was nominated in April 1996 in two categories for the 23rd Daytime Emmy Awards, the TV version of the Oscars. The network that screened the show, CBS, topped the list of nominations with a total of 69, including Outstanding Children's Specials and Outstanding Writing in a Children's Special for Keanu's documentary. At the awards ceremony on 22 May, the show gained an award for writer D. Shone Kirkpatrick.

Keanu Reeves's long-standing interest in the work of William Shakespeare had been clear throughout his career, most notably on stage in his 1985 *Romeo and Juliet* as Mercutio at Leah Posluns, and his Trinculo in *The Tempest* in 1989 at Shakespeare and Company in Mount Lennox, Massachusetts. It was Keanu who had sought out a role in Kenneth Branagh's *Much Ado About Nothing*. At the time, Keanu had expressed his interest in playing Hamlet to Branagh – with the director encouraging the young actor to pursue it.

'The first advice was to do it,' recalled Branagh of his discussions with Keanu. 'He had wondered if it would end up being a circus. He came to see me play Hamlet in the Royal Shakespeare Company and we had a long conversation. He was very gracious – the production was wonderful, it was great. And then we had a drink or two. He started to tell me what was wrong with it, and about three hours later I realised he hated the entire thing. "Well, you've got to do Hamlet, Keanu, because you obviously know how to do it – so off you go." I love him. He's a bright lad, much brighter than people think.'

Keanu's chance came through an offer from Steven Schipper, who as Artistic Director of the Manitoba Theatre Centre had auditioned Keanu for a role in the Toronto Free Theatre when the actor was sixteen. Schipper offered Keanu a slot in his Winnipeg, Canada theatre for the standard Equity fee of just under $2000 per week to play any part he wished. Keanu teamed up with director Lewis Baumander, whom he had worked with on *Romeo and Juliet*, and together the pair decided to tackle *Hamlet*.

It was an audacious move for Keanu, who had suffered at the hands of the critics for many of his movie roles, particularly his period pieces and his Shakespeare turn in *Much Ado About Nothing*. However, Keanu was serious about tackling the part, and he threw himself into the role, opting out of a major part in a Tom Clancy film, entitled *Without Remorse*, which would have earned him $6 million. He also dropped out of playing the young lead role in Michael Mann's *Heat*, alongside Al Pacino and Robert De Niro, only to be replaced by Val Kilmer, in a reversal of his *Johnny Mnemonic* experience.

Keanu had his first reunion with Baumander in February 1994, when he was in Toronto shooting *Johnny Mnemonic*. This initial discussion of the play, and the possibility of them staging it, was followed in May with a week in Winnipeg, examining the stage space available at the Manitoba Theatre Centre. After wrapping production on *A Walk in the Clouds* in October 1994, Keanu returned to Los

Keanu with his band Dogstar.

Angeles, hooked up with Baumander, and threw himself heart and soul into preparing for his debut as Hamlet the following January.

Keanu was clear in his reasons for tackling the role, and – more importantly – for doing it now, as he turned 31. 'Hamlet is the absolute role, the role of which every actor dreams. Everybody told me, "But you can't play Hamlet until you are 50!" That's false! I would have loved to have played him when I was 18. It is the part of a young man for a young actor. It is complete – love, rage, confidence, doubt, treason, desire, spirituality. To me, none of the film versions of *Hamlet* have shown this.'

A month of full cast rehearsals took place in Winnipeg in December 1994, the first chance the rest of the cast of the production had to meet their leading man. Relief, reportedly, spread throughout the company when it became clear that Keanu was not doing *Hamlet* as some movie star ego trip. It was clear from his manner and dedication to the work that he was serious about playing Hamlet. Stephen Russell, a seventeen-year veteran of the Stratford Festival, played Claudius in the production and was impressed by Keanu's preparation. 'The thing that impressed me on that first day was how much work he'd done. This was not going to be a star turn or a walk in the park. And what I realised, too, was how his principles were etched in stone. He carries a lot of weight extremely well.'

Playing up Keanu's physical strengths as an actor, director Baumander organised key scenes around him. There was no attempt, though, to simplify the language, meaning that the actor had to properly learn the entire play. Unlike in the process of movie-making, there could be no second takes if he was to dry up or fluff a line on stage – and he had 24 performances to get through in January and February 1995.

'I love the play, I love acting Shakespeare, it's the best part in Western drama,' announced Keanu, arriving in Winnipeg only to be welcomed by a 'Keanu hunt' organised by the local newspaper. The international media was not far behind, arriving in droves to chronicle his latest attempt at the Bard. Wisely, Erwin Stoff turned down all offers to film Keanu's stage performances, even denying Canadian national broadcaster CBC the chance to use clips for news reports. Clearly, Keanu's handlers were worried that their client was out of his depth with this role and were attempting to minimise the damage that making a hash of *Hamlet* could cause.

As it happened, they need not have worried so much. The first night was packed out with representatives of the international press, many waiting happily to see Keanu Reeves fall flat on his face and make a fool of himself. It was not to be, but Keanu was petrified on the night. 'One of the most horrific nights of my life, oh my gosh! I was surviving, not performing. But, it got better. It was a landmark experience for me, morally and physically. I left each night, exhausted and shattered,' admitted Keanu. While his performances were variable, opinion seemed unanimous that Keanu's Hamlet was at least not an embarrassment.

One problem Keanu had with playing the same part night after night was sticking to a consistent way of tackling it. Having little stage experience, Keanu was more used to performing for movie cameras, having several chances to interpret scenes and several takes to get it right. On stage with *Hamlet*, he could continue working like that if he really wished, but he had to do it live every night in front of an audience.

Some critics were predictably scathing, dubbing this Hamlet as 'Keanu's Excellent Adventure', of course. Several key critics, however, were astonished at how good Keanu actually was. In particular, Roger Lewis of the *Sunday Times* was immensely impressed: 'He is one of the top three Hamlets I have seen for the simple reason that he *is* Hamlet. . .full of undercurrents and overtones. He quite embodied the innocence, the splendid fury, the animal grace of the leaps and bounds, the emotional violence, that form the Prince of Denmark.'

'That was kind of him,' commented Keanu of this extremely positive notice. 'What was great was that he had seen more than one performance. It wasn't just opening night . . . I met a number of people who had never seen a play before, who said it's one of the most special events that's happened in their life, and that's right on, you know. I'll say one thing about our production – and I don't care what you think about my Hamlet – you could hear it, it made sense, it wasn't abstract, it wasn't convoluted or sensationalistic. Everyone had their place in the play and it all made sense.'

Keanu continued: 'I read *Hamlet* in high school and then I remember being shown Lawrence Olivier's *Hamlet*, but I guess the first thing that drew me was the angst – just being a teenager and having to read "To be or not to be." That was the hook that has drawn me into the path of *Hamlet*. I haven't played Romeo, or any of the larger parts in Shakespeare. I've played Mercutio and I've played Trinculo from *The Tempest*, and I did a kind of abridged Don John, so to play the second largest part in Shakespeare is a bit daunting.'

Reaction to Keanu Reeves playing Hamlet was extraordinary. The entire run of the play sold out and hotel rooms throughout Winnipeg were booked up as fans from around the world descended on the unsuspecting city. One female fan flew all the way from Australia and stayed throughout eight nightly performances.

Keanu did not ignore his fans, who queued up at the stage door afterwards in temperatures of sometimes minus 20 degrees, hoping to catch a glimpse of their movie idol. Keanu gave them more than a glimpse, often spending several hours signing autographs and chatting with fans, claiming he'd feel guilty if he didn't.

Security became an issue for the star, as his minders became worried about the fanatical nature of some of the people who were turning up outside the stage door night after night. Keanu, though, enjoyed the attention. 'So long as they don't have any knives, guns, poisons or voodoo . . . it's flattering and hopefully people like what I do. It was astonishing that some people had travelled so far. It really intensified for me that I had to put on a good show. It was great for the other actors, we had the best audiences ever. People were standing up and clapping and everyone enjoyed the piece.'

A trio of female Keanu fans from Chicago recounted their experiences on a special *Hamlet* Internet site they set up, in tribute to their screen idol. 'The Canadian immigration officer simply asked, "Are you here for the play?"' wrote one of the three.

On tour: Keanu takes his 'hobby' seriously.

'I nodded and he promptly wrote *Hamlet* on my entrance visa! We caught the closing performance, and to put it bluntly, the performance was much better than we expected! We were rewarded for our fortitude in braving the sub-sub-sub-zero temperatures with confident and capable performances that were captivating. . .we all came back with autographs, big film-developing bills, many new friends from all over the world, and a new appreciation for long underwear.'

It seemed that no matter what Keanu Reeves got up to, his loyal fans would always go the extra mile to support him in his endeavours.

Keanu Reeves had been able to indulge one of his other off-screen interests during the production of *Johnny Mnemonic* – rock music. The casting of Ice T and ex-Black Flag member Henry Rollins brought Keanu into contact with one of his rock idols. 'I know Henry Rollins through a couple of Black Flag albums,' said Keanu. 'He's such a cool cat, man. He's got some good scenes in this. We were filming in a place in Toronto, an old opera house and Henry was like, "Yeah, when we played here we tore this place up!" He's a very remarkable person.'

Keanu had taken his interest in rock 'n' roll music to the next logical stage, playing in his own band. He'd acted out the rock star role in Paula Abdul's 'Rush Rush' video. The screen star, however, decided to take a back seat in his band's musical endeavours. He plays bass in Dogstar, but is not the front man and certainly doesn't sing very often. And Dogstar did not join the thrash metal *Johnny Mnemonic* soundtrack. 'Dogstar didn't make it onto the soundtrack,' laughed Keanu. 'They left it up to the professionals.'

Although Keanu was inclined to downplay his musical ambition, what he usually termed a hobby began to take a more central role in his life – to such an extent that the actor would later forgo lucrative movie roles to go touring the world playing in Dogstar. 'Because I'm an actor and I'm playing music, I prefer the term "hobby" more,' said Keanu. 'I know musicians have career ambitions, but the ambition is to have your music heard. I have a good time. Sometimes my friends come out and sometimes they don't. Sometimes I tell them not to come. But it's good fun.'

The band had begun in 1991 when Keanu had met Robert Mailhouse, an actor in the daytime soap *Days of our Lives*, in a supermarket. Mailhouse had also featured

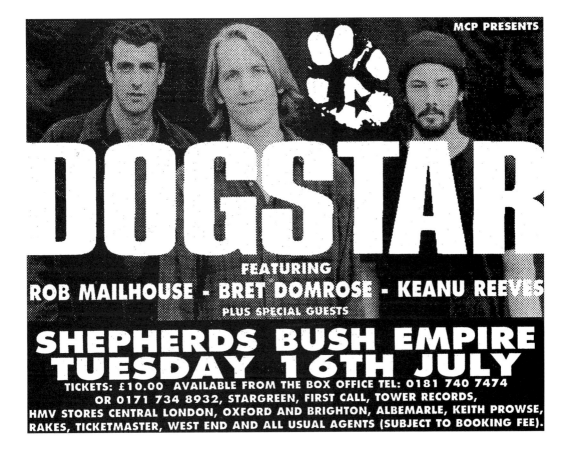

in a guest spot on *Seinfeld* as Elaine's gay boyfriend and several Aaron Spelling productions, including *Models Inc*. Keanu – ever the hockey fan – noticed Mailhouse was wearing a Detroit Redwings hockey sweater. Hooking up through hockey, the pair of new friends soon moved onto a shared interest in music, engaging in private jamming sessions. Soon Mailhouse had recruited another friend, Gregg Miller, and Dogstar was born. Mailhouse even gained extra acting work through his connection with Keanu – he's one of the executives trapped in the lift in the opening sequence of *Speed*.

'We started playing together,' recalled Keanu, claiming that the supermarket-hockey jumper story was true and not merely band-invented PR. 'He would do drums and keyboards and I would play bass.' Joined by Gregg Miller – also an actor who featured in *Who Shot Pat?* opposite Keanu's *Speed* co-star Sandra Bullock – the band practised on cover versions of Joy Division songs and others by the Grateful Dead.

Spurred on by their good vibes, the group decided to play live. 'Which was a huge mistake,' said Keanu. 'We were called Small Faecal Matter back then,' recalled Mailhouse. 'I'm surprised, actually, that for such clever lads we couldn't come up with a name,' admitted Keanu. 'We were BFS too – I called us Bull Fucking Shit or Big Fucking Sound . . .' As BFS the band played at the Roxbury, when it was considered to be LA's hot night-spot, the same night Madonna was holding a birthday party. It seems unlikely the material girl could be distracted from her revels long enough to pay much attention to the band. 'I think she was playing spin the bottle with strippers,' claimed Mailhouse. 'There we were in this tiny bar at the back and she was having this party where everyone was probably spanking each other.'

The band continued perfecting their act, joined by fourth member Bret Domrose, the most seriously musically-minded of the quartet. Soon, they'd settled on the name Dogstar, another name for Sirius, the brightest star in the sky, and became the resident band at Los Angeles' club the Troubadour. With Keanu Reeves playing in the band, their shows hardly needed to be advertised and always sold out. Dogstar would play to a venue packed with screaming teenage girls and older women with their boyfriends in tow.

People magazine was soon reporting on the phenomenon. Writer Lorraine Goods noted that Keanu was too busy concentrating on his bass playing to perform to the crowd, although the crowd seemed there to perform themselves. One unnamed 24-year-old man noted: 'It was actually better than I expected. I went because my girlfriend is in love with Keanu Reeves. It was mostly women. . .'

As the notoriety of Dogstar grew, so the Troubadour became too small to hold the screaming, bra-throwing crowds. During performances, each of the four members of the band would take turns on vocals, including at least one song from Keanu. Their original songs boasted titles like 'Ride', 'Camp' and 'Cardigan'. Keanu even tried his hand at writing songs, including 'Isabelle', about a friend's three-year-old daughter, and 'Round C'. 'That's the name of a Cheddar,' he explained to *The Face* writer Lesley O'Toole. 'But it's really about love.'

The experience of singing on stage was a different one for Keanu, who was not used to performing in public, even after his turn as Hamlet, just in front of movie technicians. 'I'm new to this,' he freely admitted. 'When I sang 'Isabelle', it was the first time this has really resembled the best part of acting. When you can feel it, your blood thrills, it's physical, your heart is open. It's emotional and sharing. . .'

By February 1995, Dogstar were venturing further afield as their following grew larger. They played at Belly Up in San Diego, before returning to Los Angeles, forgoing the Troubadour in favour of the much larger and more trendy American Legion Hall. During this period a couple of album offers were turned down by the band, worried that they might simply cash in on the novelty aspect of Keanu's participation.

In June 1995, Keanu and the others had flown off to Japan to play a six-date tour, Japan being a country where Keanu had a large and dedicated fan following. He'd featured in a commercial for Suntory Whisky to be shown exclusively in Japan. Upon returning, a six-week US tour was planned, but Mailhouse found the planned dates clashed with the shooting of a TV pilot entitled *Road Warriors*, based on the *Mad Max* movies, in which he had a featured role. When the series was not picked up, Dogstar were back in action once more. Keanu had set aside two months for Dogstar between the shooting of his next film, *Feeling Minnesota* in mid-June, and his scheduled start on *Chain Reaction* in September 1995. The Dog Days of Summer tour took in twenty US cities, ending on 18 August at the House of Blues in Los Angeles. A documentary film crew followed the band, in true *This is Spinal Tap* fashion, chronicling their backstage antics and cataloguing the attempts by Keanu's fans to get backstage and meet the actor-cum-rock-star. The director of the piece was rock video helmer and Keanu buddy Joe Charbonic.

On 29 September, the band had opened for Bon Jovi at the Forum in Los Angeles, as well as for David Bowie at the Hollywood Palladium. Then it was a trip down under for a mini-tour supporting Bon Jovi again, beginning in Auckland, New Zealand at the Supertop on 8 November, finishing off on 18th November at the Eastern Creek, in Sydney, Australia. By then the band had signed the now inevitable recording contract, with Zoo Entertainment and the BMG label. Soon there was a Dogstar fan club and official tour merchandising.

Writing in the *Sydney Morning Herald*, Katherine Tulich reviewed the performance, calling Keanu's playing 'inconsistent' and noting he left the spotlight to Bret Domrose and Robert Mailhouse, Miller having by then quit the band to pursue acting opportunities: 'Keanu shuffled coyly on the side of the stage, didn't sing, barely talked, hid most of his face under a black beanie and had his eyes on his scruffy black Doc Martens through most of Dogstar's 30-minute set of thrash grunge.'

'I admit it's pretty nerve-racking for me to go on stage,' said Keanu, 'but I'm getting more confident the more we play. I know people are coming to see me because of my cinema work, but if that brings an audience in to hear the music and gives the band a shot, then I'm grateful. We've been working really hard, practising for hours every day, so I think we're pretty good now.'

Just as momentum was beginning to build behind Dogstar and Keanu Reeves began musing aloud about seriously pursuing his musical interests by going on a world tour during the summer of 1996, Hollywood intervened, offering the actor a $10 million salary to appear alongside Sandra Bullock in *Speed 2*. Shocking many, including his own advisers, Keanu said a firm 'no', offering his desire to tour with Dogstar as the official reason for declining. Speculation mounted that there were other reasons. Since *Speed*, Keanu had been piling on the pounds, as was to be horribly evident in his next film *Chain Reaction*, and the actor couldn't face the prospect of re-entering the gym to tackle his weight problem and get back into shape. Gossip columnist Liz Smith even reported that Keanu was simply 'over' being a mega-star and was not interested in taking on a role which could cement his status as an action hero.

That left 20th Century Fox with something of a problem. Most franchise films featured the return of the same characters played by the same actors. In those where changes had been made, the characters were usually well known by the public through different sources – for example Batman in comics and on TV, or James Bond in books and movies. It was different for *Speed*, as one 20th Century Fox executive admitted to the *Los Angeles Times*. 'The characters in *Speed* were originated by these two actors, so audiences expect to see them again.' Having failed to secure the return of Keanu, however, the studio were not going to let a good franchise go to waste and set about replacing him with Jason Patric after considering *A Time to Kill* rising star Matthew McConaughey and B-movie man Billy Zane. The plot is to feature Sandra Bullock taking a trip on a cruise ship, only to have it hijacked by terrorists.

Many thought Keanu had fumbled the ball by refusing to tackle *Speed 2* and deciding to concentrate on his work with Dogstar instead, but the conventional views of Hollywood wisdom seemed to have less sway over the actor once he'd passed the age of 30.

It was during 1996 that his band were to have their biggest impact – exactly at the time that Keanu would have been shooting *Speed 2* if he'd signed on for the sequel. That summer Dogstar debuted in Europe, notably playing at Glasgow's T in the Park music festival in mid-July and a gig at London's Shepherd's Bush Empire on 16 July. Reviewing the open-air gig at Strathclyde Country Park, Pat Kane (of Scottish pop group Hue and Cry), wrote in the *Guardian*: 'When Keanu finally stumbles on stage, the screams are a symphony of the ages of woman. "Kee-ahh-noooh!" Personally, on the bodacious front, I felt short-changed. For one thing, there's some unnecessary democracy going on in Dogstar . . . [with] Keanu flailing away at his axe in semi-darkness. When he wriggles his shoulders (once), blows kisses (twice) and does his slo-mo grin (thrice), you see what a preposterously successful rock-god Keanu could be. . .'

British women's fashion magazine *Elle* sent reporter Kate Spicer to track Keanu down on his travels across Britain, beginning with his stay at Glasgow's Forte Post House hotel, where the manager commented that in person Keanu was 'just a normal guy, a nice polite man. I don't know why he always acts like a space cadet in interviews.' Spicer was not the only one on Keanu's trail, as the fan posse were also after the star, just as they'd turned up for *Hamlet* in Winnipeg. The tour bus located at T in the Park ended up being covered in pink lipstick messages including: 'Do *Speed 2* or else' and 'We love U Keanu'. The story was the same when the Dogstar crew arrived in London. Fans were soon ensconced outside the Blake Hotel, hoping to catch a glimpse of Keanu. The *Daily Record* reported that Keanu had dined at a local Indian restaurant and – in a seeming dig at his more portly state – felt obliged to report that he also snatched food from his friend's plate too.

Keanu seemed determined to play down his superstar status during the tour and play up his 'ordinary bloke' persona. He refused to do any significant press interviews while touring, and certainly didn't want to talk about Hollywood, films, or whether he'd be doing *Speed 2* or not.

Dan Thomsen, Dogstar's PR manager for the tour, emphasised that Keanu wanted to separate his movie star and rock band images. 'People keep trying to equate Keanu Reeves the movie star with the band. Nothing is going to be as big as a movie star. We've been getting really annoyed with promoters who put Keanu Reeves on the billboards.'

Grunge guru: He may be a millionaire megastar, but Keanu likes to dress down on tour with Dogstar.

While Keanu had taken his interest in playing rock 'n' roll far more seriously than Johnny Depp (who sticks to playing in his own club, the Viper Room) or Brad Pitt (who sticks to playing alone in private), the best advice anyone could offer was not to give up the day job.

There was no turning back for Keanu Reeves. He was now an A-list star in Hollywood, but it wasn't a tag he was too comfortable with. 'What is a star? A megastar? It's a word to describe people who have gleaned large success in entertainment. I don't wanna be so popular as to be recognised wherever I go. If it's something I can get around doing and still act in popular films, then I will. I'd like to hopefully do some radical, experimental, independent films.'

Throwing off the action hero mantle was top of Keanu's agenda, and he quickly lined up some low budget independent roles in *Feeling Minnesota* and *The Last Time I Committed Suicide*, but he also knew to keep his blockbuster credentials by signing up to Andrew Davis's action thriller *Chain Reaction.*

His restlessness, both personal and professional, does much to define Keanu Reeves. His unsettled nature and his wide variety of roles and films prevents him from being pigeon-holed as an actor or as a person. 'I've settled on not settling,' he boasted. 'I'm still exploring, but I'm also trying to be clear about what I can and can't do. I'm just not as developed as some other actors at my age. I'm not a producer or a director. All my energy is focused on acting. I'm limited and I'm still working to find a way inside my characters. But once you're inside, I'm learning, limitations seem to vanish.'

CHAPTER NINE

Chain Reaction

F ROLICKING in a hotel swimming pool with *Basic Instinct* star Sharon Stone was not what the tabloids expected of the man supposedly married to David Geffen, but that was the tale reported by the *Daily Mirror* in 1994 about Keanu Reeves. Thinking they finally had something to latch onto, the paper hyped up the minimal acquaintance of the two stars in steamy terms: 'Their passionate love play almost turned the pool into a sauna,' claimed the overexcited newspaper.

Later that same year, Keanu was accused by the Press of enjoying 'sleaze trips' through London's Soho during a visit to the city. Reports of 48-hour drinking and guitar playing sessions didn't live up to the banner headline 'Sleaze Trips of Hollywood Hellraiser' used by the *Daily Star*. So desperate were the papers for sordid details of Keanu's apparently non-existent private life that a relatively innocent trip to Soho became a wild fling.

By the end of 1994, the sexual confusion which surrounded the actor continued to be played both ways, making sure he didn't disappoint any of his audiences. It was the ambiguity and the lack of confirmation that allowed Keanu to succeed both as a macho action hero in *Speed* and a gay hustler in *My Own Private Idaho*, or play the title role in *Little Buddha*. His mystery was his biggest selling point.

Little over a year had passed since the Geffen story and now Keanu was linked with 23-year-old Amanda De Cadenet, with Britain's *Here* magazine describing the movie star and ex-wild child as 'Hollywood's most unlikely couple'. A spread of photos showed the couple embracing, she with a ring on her finger, as they purchased a Porsche in Los Angeles. De Cadenet, a publicity junkie, was an unlikely soulmate for publicity-shy Keanu. 'He's beautiful and sexy,' she gushed, 'but he's more than that. He's supportive and understanding.' The report, by Lisa Collins, concluded with an anonymous friend of De Cadenet's suggesting the flirtation – which had the pair shacked up in a mansion in the Hollywood Hills – would not last long. Rumours of Keanu's imminent engagement (or even secret marriage) to De Cadenet would resurface periodically through into 1997, with neither confirmation nor denial from the star himself.

Keanu was also featured prominently in an article in the magazine *Buzz*, focusing on 'Himbos', the male equivalent of the Bimbo – brainless but gorgeous-looking. Writer Deborah Michel noted: 'Keanu's mind-boggling blankness doesn't detract from his appeal in the slightest. On the contrary, it *is* his appeal. . .'

Engaged or not? Keanu with Amanda De Cadanet, the subject of romantic rumours.

Confounding all expectations of him, the next movie Keanu Reeves committed to was a low budget love story entitled *Feeling Minnesota*. The script was by 34-year-old unknown Steven Baigelman, who had developed his project at Robert Redford's Sundance Institute. Signing onto the film before *Speed* became a hit and Keanu's asking price was to jump from around $1.5 million to $7 million per film, Keanu was to be paid about $200,000 for his role in the $10 million film. Willing to take a huge reduction in pay for what he regarded as a role he would not normally be considered for, Keanu showed his willingness to put his artistic ambitions before his earning power.

'I don't know what it was that clicked between us,' said writer-director Baigelman, 'but we hit it off. Couple of days later he committed. Couple of days after that, *Speed* opened and went through the roof. He had committed verbally but hadn't signed.

'I can't believe how little money he took,' claimed Baigelman of Keanu's $200,000 salary. 'He did it for lunch money. Keanu has said he came to audition, but from my point of view he did not audition – we met. But that's a clue as to why he became involved – he doesn't think like a movie star. He's an actor, and he thinks about what's going to excite him.'

Feeling Minnesota told the story of two estranged brothers, Sam (Vincent D'Onofrio) and Jjaks (Keanu) – whose name is the legacy of a typographical mistake on his birth certificate. Jjaks is released from prison just in time to attend Sam's wedding, where he falls in love with his brother's bride-to-be, Freddie

(Cameron Diaz). When Jjaks discovers a local Seattle mobster is punishing Freddie by forcing her to marry Sam, the pair decide to run off together, stealing a fortune Sam has ripped off from the mobster. The film builds to an inevitably bloody and tragic climax in Las Vegas.

At first, Keanu was worried about the dark nature of the script, but persuaded to read through it again by Baigelman, he saw that his part allowed him a return to the kind of characters he had played in *River's Edge* and *My Own Private Idaho*. 'When I first read it I didn't like it at all. I found it very harsh,' said Keanu. *Feeling Minnesota* was certainly a million miles away from *Speed*, but he decided it was a role he was suited to. Keanu's other co-stars on the film were to be Dan Aykroyd, Tuesday Weld and Courtney Love. Shooting began during April 1995 with the production wrapping in June in Las Vegas.

Keanu and Cameron Diaz hit it off – and had to cope with difficult sex scenes which they would shoot with about 30 people standing around watching. On the first day Diaz came to work, she had to shoot a scene in which she has sex with Keanu in the bathroom. 'That was like, "Hi, my name is Cameron, let's fuck . . ." But Keanu and I got along well. He's a strange cat, but he's a cool guy. He's in his head a lot. He comes on and he goes off, and you just try to get in front of him and be the target and then try to duck out of the way. He is a very sweet guy with a heart of gold.'

Low budget endeavours: Keanu with Cameron Diaz on the set of Feeling Minnesota.

Keanu couldn't escape the critical disappointment with Feeling Minnesota.

Baigelman had to face directing Keanu in this, his first full-blown movie sex scene. 'It's more difficult for the actors than for me. These are two really hot people who have some attraction for each other – they like each other as people. They knew their parts, knew their scenes, and I shot the sex scenes very basically. It's not *Red Shoe Diaries*. The most difficult part was keeping Keanu's thing inside the jock. If it fell out, he'd put it back and go on. . .Keanu and Cameron looked like they were enjoying themselves.'

The cast and crew weren't the only people around. The Keanu Reeves fan club turned up on location in Minneapolis, with about 100 or so teenage girls hanging around for hours hoping for a glimpse of their idol. Keanu would find himself tied down to signing autographs for about an hour at a time – something he was happy to do, as he'd shown during his run in *Hamlet*. On set he was quiet and polite to everyone. One production assistant commented to *Premiere* magazine: 'He sort of keeps to himself and that's kinda admirable – it's not like he needs to be the centre of attention.'

Released in America in September, *Feeling Minnesota* was not welcomed by critics. *Entertainment Weekly* was disappointed, awarding the film a 'D' rating. 'Keanu Reeves and Vincent D'Onofrio, as brothers locked in a clash of destiny, snarl, glower, and, mostly, beat each other up, so that we come away from almost every scene pummelled by their Midwestern Cain-and-Abel fury.'

Similarly the *San Francisco Chronicle* thought Reeves was not at his best. 'Reeves hasn't a clue how to convey irony or depth. Give this guy a buzz cut, an Uzi and a blank expression and he's fine – as he proved in his best movie, *Speed*. Otherwise he's stiff and hopeless.'

Rachel Weisz, Keanu and Morgan Freeman tackle Chain Reaction.

Having avoided *Speed 2*, Keanu Reeves was tempted back into action hero mode for *Chain Reaction*, an action-adventure film to be directed by Andrew Davis, the man behind the Oscar-winning movie update of the TV series *The Fugitive*. Put back from a September 1995 start to January 1996 to fit in with Keanu's schedule, *Chain Reaction* used a rather unusual location for much of the film: Argonne's Continuous Wave Deuterium Demonstrator (CWDD) in Chicago, built by the Army for ground-based 'Star Wars' research, but never activated as the Strategic Defence Initiative programme was cancelled by Congress just as the facility was completed.

By the time Keanu Reeves had signed on to the film, Argonne was buzzing with anticipation. When the actor actually showed up for a tour of the facility, the office grapevine worked overtime, with employees soon lining the corridors hoping for a glimpse of Keanu, and local newspaper reporters began calling up to ask if it were true Keanu was visiting the facility. In contrast, when Morgan Freeman, co-starring in the movie, turned up, he was more interested in discussing the physics behind the film with Argonne's chemists.

In the film Keanu plays Eddie Kasalivich, a technician who is helping a University of Chicago physicist Dr Alistair Barkley (Nicholas Rudall) develop a radical new way to create energy from mere water. Having developed and demonstrated this new technology, Keanu's idealist is ready to make a worldwide announcement, but darker forces have other ideas. When the physicist is killed, the lab destroyed and Keanu is framed for the crime, he goes on the run with a young English student Dr Lily Sinclair (Rachel Wiesz) for company. When the student is kidnapped by the bad guys, Keanu traces them to an underground lab in Virginia, the setting for the explosive climax.

Nowhere to run: Rachel Wiesz and Keanu in Chain Reaction.

Keanu – long-haired and unshaven, as well as somewhat chubbier than his *Speed* persona – described his character of Eddie as 'a kind of intuitive machinist. I don't have a physics degree or anything like that. The back story is that I grew up in the steel mills working with my father, who was working tending the mill. He is the kind of guy who had to fix everything, to maintain everything, and I grew up around that. My formal education is behind my practical education.' To prepare for the role Keanu 'spent some time with physicists', met with a CIA agent and 'read a bit about Buckminster Fuller', whose book *Critical Path* was an inspiration for *Chain Reaction*.

Bearing in mind the effect that teaming Sandra Bullock with Keanu had on her career in *Speed*, actress Rachel Wiesz was glad to be teamed with Keanu in this new film. 'It's not primarily a love story. Our relationship is we get thrown together; we don't know each other at all in the beginning. . .,' explained Wiesz, 'I've only been in the country for six months. I'm very English and he is very Chicago. . . .'

Both Keanu and Wiesz suffered for their art on *Chain Reaction*, shooting on Chicago locations in sub-zero temperatures. 'It's the hardest film I've ever done,' claimed Keanu. 'It was cold, but we had good support standing by. It's hard to conjure up emotions in that cold.' Weisz recalled temperatures falling as low as minus 44 degrees, and Davis admitted that the production was shut down at one stage by local fire crews, due to health and safety concerns. Despite the heaters lugged to each location and the gloves and winter-wear supplied, it just got too cold to continue filming.

As on *Feeling Minnesota*, the Keanu Reeves fan club turned out to see their idol in action. Filming in January at Mandel Hall on the University of Chicago campus used about 1000 extras to fill a lecture hall – many of whom had come specifically to see Keanu. Several students boasted to the local newspaper of having obtained Keanu's autograph. Many fans posted their experiences as extras on the film on the Internet, in the same way that fans had reviewed Keanu's turn in *Hamlet*. Their comments were interesting, with die-hard fans calling Keanu 'kinda beefy looking. He has a double chin'; 'longer hair than we've seen for a while'; 'I came away even more impressed by Keanu's acting abilities'; and 'he looked frustrated and a bit distracted'.

The explosive, action sequence centrepiece of the film – the *Chain Reaction* equivalent to the spectacular train crash in *The Fugitive* – was Keanu's dramatic escape on a motorbike from an exploding laboratory. The scene sees Keanu returning to the lab after a party, only to discover the physicist he's helping is dead and the lab is about to explode. He zooms off on his motorbike, only to escape the blast and shockwave by skidding into a sandpit. It was a sequence that returned Keanu to his action man mode, but also allowed him to indulge his off-screen love of motorbikes.

Knowing he would get to keep the bike after filming, Keanu was asked by the production what kind of bike it should be. The actor settled on a 1976 KZ1000 Kawasaki, painted dull black for the film.

In the climax of the sequence, just as the shockwave seems about to envelop Keanu, the motorcycle skids into a sandpit as the explosion sends an unfortunate oil tanker hurtling over his head. Keanu surfaces to check out the smouldering ruins, a desolate area covering eight city blocks – provided through miniature models and clever computer graphics work.

Keanu plays a minor role in The Last Time I Committed Suicide.

Finally released in September 1996 in America and November in Britain, *Chain Reaction* was broadly welcomed as a fast-paced, imaginative action-flick. *Entertainment Weekly* took to the 'crisply-shot' film and felt Keanu had 'become a confident and likeable action star', but thought he 'needs a script that does more than pair him with a pretty physicist (Rachel Weisz) and blueprint a repetitive series of escapes'. It was for the action sequences, explosions, bridge-stunts and iceboat chases that *Chain Reaction* would be chiefly remembered.

Keanu Reeves was setting a pattern for his film roles which looked as though it would sustain him through his 30s. Combining action roles in something like *Speed* or *Chain Reaction* with a more character-based, low-budget, indie-type film like *Feeling Minnesota* allowed Keanu to maintain his bankable Hollywood presence and to experiment and stretch himself. With that aim in mind, he took a small role in a small film immediately after completing *Chain Reaction. The Last Time I Committed Suicide* was a very low-budget period piece set in the 1940s. The $2 million film featured Thomas Jane as young beatnik Neal Cassady in the tale of how Jack Kerouac came to write *On the Road*. First time writer-director Stephen Kay had written the script for the film in consultation with the widow of Neal Cassady, a friend of Kerouac's, whose letters had spurred the writer into action. Keanu played Neal's best friend, Harry, and was taking some risk in this part, as at the time he made it the movie was without a distributor, and so was not guaranteed a release. Nevertheless, the small part in a potentially obscure movie suited his new strategy. The film premiered at the Sundance Film Festival in January 1997, and was called a 'grand achievement in style and subtlety' by Rebecca Yeldham in the programme. A limited, America cinema release was tentatively scheduled for *The Last Time I Committed Suicide* in June 1997, preceded by a pay-per-view debut on cable service Cinemax in April.

Other parts came Keanu's way, but even when he agreed to feature in them there was no guarantee the films would ever get made. Warner Brothers offered Keanu $9 million ($2 million more than his *Chain Reaction* pay packet) to star in a big budget sci-fi epic called *Soldier*. Keanu was to play an itinerant warrior who is forced to become a hero and defend a band of settlers on a remote planet. With a good creative team involved, *Soldier* looked like it would happen eventually, with or without Keanu. The script was written by David Webb Peoples (*Blade Runner, Unforgiven* and *12 Monkeys*) and was to be directed by Paul (*Mortal Kombat*) Anderson.

Such was the prospect of securing Keanu's services for a film that studios even bought up material with the star in mind for the lead role. 20th Century Fox secured Howard Blum's 12-page treatment *Men of Honor* for $400,000 solely because they felt it contained a good role for Keanu. *Men of Honor* deals with a journalist whose life is threatened when he gets involved with a man in the Federal witness protection programme and finds himself becoming a Mafia target.

An on-again, off-again project was another first time writer-director-led film that interested Keanu. *Voyeur: A Divine Comedy* was the brainchild of 33-year-old Rupert Wyatt, a France-based British film-maker who had made only short films previously. Wyatt based his script on Dante's original, and secured commitments from a starry cast. He persuaded Keanu to consider the character of 'Gluttony', assistant to Jean-Claude Dreyfus. The story concerned a novelist who enters the

In the pay of the devil: Keanu worked alongside Al Pacino in the fantasy-tinged thriller Devil's Advocate.

Parisian underworld to research his new book, only to be caught up with characters representing the Seven Deadly Sins. As well as Keanu, Wyatt had Geraldine Chaplin as Pride and F. Murray Abraham as Lucifer. Shooting was scheduled for October 1996 in France for eight weeks at a budget of 23 million francs (about $5 million). Unfortunately, the deal securing Keanu's services for the film fell through, and it looked unlikely that the project would ever get off the ground, due to problems with the financing.

Another project to which Keanu became attached at the end of 1996 was *Devil's Advocate*, a thriller from Warner Brothers in which a young lawyer joins a fancy law firm, only to discover he's actually working for the Devil. The lead part in this movie seemed to have been offered to every young actor in Hollywood, including Christian Slater, Johnny Depp and Brad Pitt. This time the movie was a go, with shooting beginning in October 1996 in New York. Taylor Hackford was behind the camera as director, and co-starring with Keanu was Al Pacino, (as the Devil, no less) and Charlize Theron (from *Two Days in the Valley*) as his wife. As on *Feeling Minnesota*, Keanu's manager Erwin Stoff was on board as an executive producer.

The film had been in development for eight years, since Warner's Vice President Rob Guralnick had optioned the Andrew Neiderman novel when he first came to work for the studio. The film had entered pre-production once before, with Joel Schumacher (*Batman Forever*, *A Time to Kill*) signed up as director. With Stoff looking out for his client's interests, *Devil's Advocate* looked set to be a better vehicle for Keanu than *Chain Reaction* had turned out to be.

In early October Keanu spent some time in a Florida courtroom to research his role in *Devil's Advocate*, wearing a sober suit and a tie for his visits to the public gallery. When shooting began in New York, the Keanu sightings began almost immediately, with the star being spotted around town, dining out and visiting the theatre for a performance of *A Delicate Balance* on Broadway.

Everything was not sweetness and light on location for *Devil's Advocate*, as the film slipped behind schedule, due – according to reports – to friction between co-stars Keanu Reeves and Al Pacino. Pacino, who had praised his young co-star on *Donnie Brasco*, Johnny Depp, was said to be none too impressed with Keanu's acting abilities. In addition, both Pacino and Keanu were said to have had disputes with director Taylor Hackford over the direction the movie was taking. Talking to the *Los Angeles Times*, Warner Brothers spokesman Rob Friedman maintained that the film was only a day or two over schedule and that everything on set was fine. Through a spokesman, Pacino was reported to have stated: 'I look forward to seeing Keanu every day. He's a joy to work with . . .'

Rumours during the *Devil's Advocate* shoot even had Keanu joining Alcoholics Anonymous and attending group meetings in New York. While he claimed not to have a drinking problem, Keanu did admit to having given up the bottle for the duration of the film, believing it was necessary for maintaining the 'clear-eyed' look he hoped to put across as the idealistic young lawyer.

Before he'd even finished *Devil's Advocate*, Keanu had lined up his first role for 1997 – playing a gay man who falls in love with a woman. Offered the starring role in *Object of My Affection*, scripted by Wendy Wasserstein, Keanu was lined up to work again with his *Dangerous Liaisons* co-star Uma Thurman as the woman who turns his head. Director Nicholas Hynter, previously a star stage director of the Royal Shakespeare Company, was a major factor in Keanu's interest. Since his film of Alan Bennett's play *The Madness of King George*, Hynter had gone on to make the film of *The Crucible* with Winona Ryder and Daniel Day-Lewis. Notably absent from comment on Keanu's new role was his manager Erwin Stoff, who some felt might be worried about his client's decision to abandon his *Speed*-style action hero status.

As he entered his mid-30s, Keanu Reeves had three interests he indulged seriously: acting, Dogstar and motorbikes. Between his summer tours of 1995 and 1996 with Dogstar, Keanu had taken a break from the band to shoot *Chain Reaction*. After the film, Dogstar was again to occupy the actor. An album, entitled *Our Little Visionary*, was tentatively scheduled for release in May 1997, after having been delayed a couple of times, produced by Ramones and Talking Heads producer Ed Stasium. An 'enhanced' four track CD entitled *Quattro Formaggi* (*Four Cheeses*), which included video clips of the band playable on a computer as well as the music playable on a CD, had been released in July 1996.

The band also played the Dragonfly, a Los Angeles club, under the assumed name 'Sixpack' – a gimmick to see whether people were coming to see the band just for Keanu. The actor invited friends to this performance, including his *Bill and Ted* and *Freaked* co-star Alex Winter. 'We played in this bar and there were about fifty people, most of them our friends,' admitted Keanu. 'It was funny. Our guitarist had nineteen people on his guest list. I made fun of him, but I guess we were lucky, because if he hadn't brought them, there wouldn't have been anyone there. . .'

There was friction between Al Pacino and Keanu during the shooting of Devil's Advocate.

Despite missing out on film roles and despite the advice of Erwin Stoff and his other managers, Keanu insisted on pursuing his interest in Dogstar. 'I don't want to become a rock star. This is not a second career, or anything like that. I'm an actor. Playing music and hanging out with friends is a really good time. Right now, I'm just a bass player. I like the physicality of it, the way it feels to play the bass.' His musical influences were widespread, as shown by the CD collection he took on tour with Dogstar in Europe. The titles included Miles Davis, Jesus and Mary Chain, Hole (featuring his *Feeling Minnesota* co-star Courtney Love), Sonic Youth, Coltrane, Gorecki's Third Symphony and others.

Keanu's other love, his motorbikes, had already caused him to have a brush with death, left him permanently scarred and caused him much grief. Before the secret Dogstar/Sixpack gig, Keanu had taken another serious tumble on Monday 27 May 1996 at about 9pm in Los Angeles. Heading West on Sunset, Keanu swerved his bike to avoid a car that pulled out from the kerb, only to smash into another and fly through the air, landing on the road, where other cars swerved to avoid hitting the actor.

Keanu managed to get to his feet, only to discover his ankle was broken. When the police arrived on the scene, they confirmed the teen idol actor was alert, in pain, but smiling. He was taken to hospital two blocks from the accident, where staff claimed he was more concerned about the state of his bike than with the state of himself.

After examination, Keanu was told he had a broken right ankle with bone fragments, multiple contusions and abrasions as well as some chipped teeth. He had to have surgery to remove the fragments before they could migrate and cause further problems.

It was the worst accident Keanu had suffered since his Topanga Canyon crash several years earlier. He was released from hospital – in a cast and on crutches – on Wednesday 29 May. By the end of the same day, he was back in the studio recording with Dogstar and then performing on stage at the Dragonfly, where Alex Winter had been surprised to see Keanu limp on to stage with his leg in a cast and play the set leaning on a bar stool.

Keanu's primary interest in his life was acting – not stardom and fame, but acting. 'I've been very lucky in my career to do so many different kinds of roles. It's something I try to do as much as possible, to expand my range. I've been lucky to have the opportunities. I don't know how Hollywood sees it. Now someone like Tom Cruise – he's a movie star in the old-fashioned tradition.'

Whatever he might have thought – Keanu Reeves is without doubt a modern movie star. The success of the blockbuster *Speed* and the money-making *Bill and Ted* films ensured that his reputation as an earner for the studios outlived flops like *Johnny Mnemonic* and critical misfires like *Little Buddha*.

Despite preferring acting to fame, Keanu is clear that much benefit has flowed from being famous. His ability to look after his sister Kim before her cancer went into remission came directly from his earnings as a movie star. 'It gives me the opportunity for freedom,' admitted Keanu about his money.

Working for himself was something Keanu was moving towards, following his new-found status in Hollywood. Never before in his career had he worked with material he had developed specifically for himself, being content instead to be available for hire. 'If I can come up with some cool stories and get people to help

Amanda de Cadenet has struck up a romance with Keanu Reeves

Engagement rings, expensive gifts –

are Keanu and Amanda in love?

Keanu Reeves seems an odd match for maneater Amanda de Cadenet, but the...

More than just friends
Keanu has been living with Amanda

A very public embrace
The normally reclusive Keanu does not seem to care who sees him cuddling her

Already Keanu is playing by Amanda's rules
The man once declared: 'I don't need material possessions' has just bought a £60,000 Porsche under Amanda's watchful eye

Sharon's sexy sizzler in pool with Keanu

HOPES FADING FOR DJ KENNY

Reeves and de Cadenet

witched's Elizabeth Montgomery: a tribute

People weekly

Cool, mysterious
KEANU REEVES
Life is an excellent adventure for a star who has no home, no Special Someone and no rival as Hollywood's most enigmatic sex symbol

THEIR STEAMY KISSES RAISE TEMPERATURES

Success not on a plate

MUCH ADO ABOUT KEANU

Adrift and adored, Keanu Reeves is Hollywood's hunk of the hour, proving that *Speed* doesn't kill

O ONE KNEW THE GUY IN THE dirty wool cap and battered shin pads who... rigged-bus act...

VANITY FAIR

AUGUST 1995
£2.40

OUTBREAK IN THE JUNGLE
Blood and Death on the Front Lines of the Ebola-Virus Nightmare
by Laurie Garrett

DOMINICK DUNNE ON THE O.J. TRIAL

THE CHAOS IN WOMEN'S TENNIS
by Frank Deford

CARLY SIMON'S MOTHER LOAD
Scenes from Her Tortured Family Album
by Marie Brenner

$200 MILLION UNDER THE SEA
The Inside Story of Kevin Costner's Disaster-Prone Waterworld
by Charles Fleming

The Wild One
KEANU REEVES ON SEX, HOLLYWOOD AND LIFE ON THE RUN
by Michael Shnayerson

PLUS: The Shawcross Legacy, Bob Woodward's Significant Other Writing Partner and the Stars of Malibu East

S uddenly the rumor of Keanu and David Geffen was everywhere. Like Richard Gere and gerbils.

K eanu goes from project to project with one interruption now, if money. Whether or not he is ever pleased with his work is unclear. "One of the things that locked us together," says Robert Longo, director of *Johnny Mnemonic*, "was that I'd think everything was bad." Every shot could be better. "Keanu would go off and keep doing the scene, too, thinking it could be better." Robert Kurtzm, the storeworker for *A Walk in the Clouds*, puts it more bluntly. "He gets angry at himself," Kurtzm says. "He just doesn't think his acting is very good."

"There are days when I'm O.K.," Keanu says. But not too many. "Maybe it's because I'm a Virgo, it's in my sign to be hard on myself."

In his downtime on the sets of *Johnny Mnemonic* and *A Walk in the Clouds*, Keanu could often be found muttering Shakespeare. It was no mere exercise: he had committed to take on theater's greatest challenge at the end of his busiest year ever. Nearly a year ahead of time, Keanu agreed to block out two months for the production, at less than $2,000 a week. *Speed's* success made the sacrifice specific: he had to turn down four movies, including *Heat*, with Robert De Niro and Al Pacino. "Yeah," he says. "But . . . *Hamlet.*"

Keanu went about with his suitcase to Winnipeg in early December for the start of rehearsals. He found a city giddy with anticipation. One local paper announced a daily Keanu watch. For the play's sold-out run, hand-woven seats booked for Keanuphiles, mostly women, from all over the world; one woman flew all the way from Australia to sit through eight performances.

Among the cast of professional Shakespeareans, there may have lurked a doubt as to the recklessness of their leading man. The doubts were soon dispelled. "The (Continued on page 112)

... who keeps people guessing: about his home (lately, a room in a Hollywood hotel); his love life (he has had only one steady in his life); even how he came to have his passion for acting. "I don't know anything, man," Reeves once said when asked about his craft. "I don't know what I'm saying..."

...story by William Gibson, Reeves stars as a 21st-century smuggler who downloads data into a computer chip implanted in his brain—and winds up with a deadly headache. Though it will surely send a chill down the electronic spine of the nation's cyberpunks, the movie is not up to *Speed*; indeed, one way is...

"Oh I miss...

me develop them for me . . . I would love to tell the Edward DeVere story. He was the 17th century Earl of Oxford, who is considered to be one of the possible authors of Shakespeare's work. For me, it would be great to play this and illuminate the Elizabethan life, the Elizabethan drama, because to me that's the closest we've come to the Greeks. However, no one is going to care and it's never going to happen.'

If he can't get his own passionate projects off the ground, it seems like Keanu Reeves will only be as good (or as bad) as the roles he chooses to play. It has to be hoped he has learned from his own past. He needs to pursue more roles like those in *River's Edge, Point Break, My Own Private Idaho, Speed, A Walk in the Clouds* and *Feeling Minnesota*. In these films Keanu has successfully explored a variety of roles, including action heroes, romantic leads and offbeat, oddball characters and he's turned in creditable performances in all of them. Where he has had problems has been in costume dramas like *Dangerous Liaisons, Bram Stoker's Dracula* and *Little Buddha* (which doesn't bode well for his Edward DeVere idea), and in weird flops like *Even Cowgirls Get the Blues, Freaked* and *Johnny Mnemonic*. For Keanu his success lies not so much in the performance, but in his choice of roles.

Keanu has strong ideas about selecting parts: 'It's really the script and the part and then who's working on it. It's about what you can find and what comes your way. I'd like to be able to work in both mainstream and independent film, and to do theatre. I'd love to act in another language, too. I'd like to speak French and Italian, ancient Greek or Latin.'

Keanu told *Premiere* magazine, 'I can't say I've been totally different from other actors my age. I mean, I've always played the kind of male equivalent of the female ingenue. I've always played innocents. That has been a recurring theme throughout my career. There's only been a few instances where I didn't play that role. *I Love You to Death* was one example, and *Speed*, and maybe *My Own Private Idaho*. My career through-line is innocence, in a variety of different genres. I think I've done some good work in some films. I think I'm an acquired taste. I think my acting changes pretty much, but you either dig me or you don't. More than a lot of actors, my public persona has really coloured the interpretation of my work.'

The actor recognised the downside of his determination to remain a private individual. 'You can't get any more ridiculous, I guess, than being married to a man you don't know. That's pretty good, pretty good. It's not my acting that gave me the reputation, but my press. I'm a pretty wacky, goofy guy and I think I've been chastised by my personality, pigeon-holed because of who I am or who they perceive me to be, or the way that I was. I make excellent short copy because I use words like "excellent". I'm just trying not to see any of that and just concentrate on work and life.'

Keanu had even become the subject of other artists' works, including a series of watercolours of 'Keanu Sightings' by 28-year-old Southern Californian artist Keith Mayerson, as well as magic lanterns featuring the actor, shown in 1996 as part of the *Pure Beauty* show at LA's Museum of Contemporary Art. Mayerson had given considerable thought to the role Keanu plays in contemporary culture. 'He assumes the masculine role in films, but it's not an aggressive masculinity, like Clint Eastwood. He's always passive, like in *Speed* where he runs around catching balls other people throw at him.' According to Mayerson, Keanu is always the seduced, never the seducer.

The media fascination with Keanu even extended to academia. In 1994 the Art Centre College of Design in Pasadena, California added a new course to its series of studies on Fassbinder, Pasolini and Godard – *The Films of Keanu Reeves.*

Instructor Stephen Prina felt that Keanu's body of work was perfectly able to sustain academic study. 'He has a peculiar detachment that doesn't allow for the kind of relationship you have with a traditional method actor.'

Keanu himself felt the course was a bizarre development. 'I found out about that through somebody who had actually gone to the school a couple of years before and was familiar with the instructor,' said Keanu, 'so, it wasn't like, "There's a course about you." The teacher generally works with directors and what he does is take someone's work and use it as a jumping-off point for a variety of other topics. He would say: "Comedy and drama from *Bill and Ted* . . . let's look at Nietzsche and the birth of tragedy." He uses these films or this actor as a flashpoint for going off in different directions of study, whether it be theory or philosophy, sociological or semiotic, and I was told he used my past career because of its variety in genre and director. It was funny, I guess, and curious. . .'

Keanu's still-strong connections with his sisters Kim and Karina (who went on the 1996 European tour with Dogstar) and his mother Patricia made up for the absence of his father in his life. In the summer of 1996 his father had been released from prison, desperate for a reunion with his famous son. 'I put drugs before my children,' Samuel Nowlin Reeves lamented, 'but I want to be forgiven.' The hurt Samuel had caused the young Keanu Reeves was not so easily forgiven and Keanu refused to see his newly released father.

The childhood that Keanu had experienced was not materially poor, but emotionally turbulent. The lack of a steady father-figure resulted in Keanu's inability to sustain his own relationships, and a rootless existence. 'It's just something that happened,' said Keanu of his apparent homelessness. Although he'd bought properties for others, including sister Kim, Keanu had never invested in a home for himself, preferring instead to live out of a suitcase when on location with films or in the infamous Chateau Marmont, site of John Belushi's drug overdose on Sunset Strip. It was a habit that Keanu showed no sign of changing.

Some habits Keanu had changed. He'd made no secret of his dabbling in drugs, but after the death of his friend River Phoenix drug-taking was something Keanu determined to avoid. The death of his friend had been a shock, and even though Keanu put it down to 'a mistake' or 'an accident', it opened his eyes. It also served as a warning for his addiction to speeding on his motorbikes. His Topanga Canyon crash and the May 1996 smash on Sunset Strip had resulted in Keanu slowing his own speed. His broken ankle proved to be a considerable nuisance when on tour with Dogstar during the summer of 1996, a hassle the actor-cum-rock-star didn't want to have to deal with. There were ever increasing signs that Keanu had finally left the 'airhead' behind.

Well-read (his favourite authors are science fiction writer Philip K. Dick, Dostoevsky, T.S. Eliot and works of Greek mythology) and clearly smarter than he comes across in interviews, whether in print or on television, Keanu Reeves hides behind a handy Hollywood persona. 'I'm Mickey [Mouse],' he once said. 'They don't know who's inside the suit.' It's a persona that has probably reached the end of its usefulness, as Keanu moves into a new, more mature phase in his career.

'It hasn't changed since I began,' claimed Keanu. 'You're always auditioning, you're looking for work, the struggle never changes. You read scripts, you have meetings. I'm just trying to work and make good films and perform well.'

Filmography

Early Work
Romeo and Juliet (Stage)
Wolfboy (Stage)
Hangin' In (Episode of Canadian TV series)
Night Heat (TV movie, bit part)

Advertisements
Coke (TV advertisement)
Suntory (Japanese TV advertisement)

Theatre
Hamlet (Winnipeg, Canada, 1994)

Films
Youngblood (1986)
USA 1986 109 minutes
Directed by Peter Markle
Screenplay by Peter Markle and John Whitmore
Production Company: Metro-Goldwyn-Mayer/United
Artists/Guber-Peters
Cast: Rob Lowe (Dean Youngblood), Cynthia Gibb
(Jessie Chadwick), Patrick Swayze (Derek Sutton), Ed
Lauter (Murray Chadwick), Jim Youngs (Kelly
Youngblood), Eric Nesterenko (Blane Youngblood),
Keanu Reeves (Hiver)

Young Again (1986, TV)
(AKA I Wish I Were 18 Again)
USA 1986 100 minutes
Directed by Steven Hilliard Stern
Screenplay by Barbara Hall, Story by David Simon
Production Company: Disney
Cast: Jack Gilford (Old Man), Keanu Reeves (Michael
Riley, 17), Jessica Steen (Tracy Gordon), Robert Urich
(Michael Riley, 40), Lindsay Wagner (Laura Gordon)

Act of Vengeance (1986, TV)
USA 1986 95 minutes
Directed by John Mackenzie
Screenplay by Scott Spencer, based upon the book by
Trevor Armbrister

Production Company: Lorimar Motion Pictures
Cast: Charles Bronson (Jock Yablonski), Ellen Burstyn
(Margaret Yablonski), Wilford Brimley (Tony Boyle),
Hoyt Axton (Silous Huddleston), Robert Schenkkan
(Paul Gilly), Ellen Barkin (Annette Gilly),
Keanu Reeves (Buddy Martin)

Under the Influence (1986, TV)
USA 1986 100 minutes
Directed by Thomas Carter
Screenplay by Joyce Reberta-Burditt
Production Company: CBS Entertainment Productions
Cast: Dana Andersen (Terri Talbot), Paddi Edwards
(Eve), Andy Griffith (Noah Talbot), Season Hubley
(Ann Talbot Simpson), Richard Lawson (Dr Duran),
Paul Provenza (Stephen Talbot), Keanu Reeves (Eddie
Talbot)

Trying Times: Moving Day (1986, PBS)
USA 1986 60 minutes

Brotherhood of Justice (1986, TV)
USA 1986 97 minutes (94, Europe)
Directed by Charles Braverman
Written by Jeffrey Bloom, story by Noah Jubelirer
Production Company: Margot Winchester Productions
Cast: Keanu Reeves (Derek), Kiefer Sutherland (Victor),
Lori Loughlin (Christie), Joe Spano (Bob Grootemat),
Darren Dalton (Scottie), Evan Mirand (Mule), Don
Michael Paul (Collin)

Babes in Toyland (1986, TV)
USA 1986 150 minutes
Directed by Clive Donner
Based on work by Victor Herbert (operetta), Glen
McDonough (operetta)
Production Company: Neil T. Maffeo/Bavaria Film Studios
Cast: Drew Barrymore (Lisa Piper), Eileen Brennan
(Mrs Piper/Widow Hubbard), Googy Gress
(Jim/Georgie Porgie), Pat Morita (The Toymaster),
Richard Mulligan (Bernie/Barnaby Barnacle), Keanu

Reeves (Alex/Jack Be Nimble)

Flying (1986)
(AKA Dream to Believe)
Canada 1986 94 minutes
Directed by Paul Lynch
Screenplay by John Sheppard
Production Company: Brightstar Films
Cast: Olivia D'Abo (Robin), Sean McCann (Jack),
Renee Murphy (Leah), Keanu Reeves (Tommy), Jessica
Steen (Cindy), Rita Tushingham (Jean)

River's Edge (1986)
USA 1986 99 minutes
Directed by Tim Hunter
Screenplay by Neal Jimenez
Production Company: Hemdale Film Corporation
Cast: Crispin Glover (Layne), Keanu Reeves (Matt),
Ione Skye [as Ione Skye Leitch] (Clarissa), Daniel
Roebuck (Samson), Dennis Hopper (Feck), Joshua
John Miller (Tim), Roxana Zal (Maggie), Josh Richman
(Tony), Phil Brock (Mike), Tom Bower (Bennett),
Constance Forslund (Madeleine)

The Prince of Pennsylvania (1988)
USA 1988 87 minutes
Directed by Ron Nyswaner
Screenplay by Ron Nyswaner
Production Company: New Line
Cast: Bonnie Bedelia (Pam Marshetta), Tracey Ellis
(Lois Sike), Jeff Hayenga (Jack Sike), Amy Madigan
(Carla Headlee), Keanu Reeves (Rupert Marshetta), Jay
O. Sanders (Trooper Joe), Fred Ward (Gary Marshetta)

Permanent Record (1988)
USA 1988 91 minutes
Directed by Marisa Silver
Screenplay by Jarre Fees, Larry Ketron, Alice Liddle
Production Company: Paramount Pictures
Cast: Pamela Gidley (Kim), Alan Boyce (David
Sinclair), Michael Elgert (Jake), Jennifer Rubin
(Lauren), Michelle Meyrink (M.G.), Keanu Reeves
(Chris Townsend), Phil Diskin (Security Guard), Lou
Reed (himself), Garrett Lambert (Producer), Richard
Bradford (Leo Verdell), Carolyn Tomei (Chemistry
Teacher), Dakin Matthews (Mr McBain)

The Night Before, (1988)
USA 1988 85 minutes
Directed by Thom Eberhardt
Screenplay by Thom Eberhardt and Gregory Scherick
Production Company: Kings Road
Entertainment/Zealcorp Productions Limited
Cast: Keanu Reeves (Winston Connelly), Lori Loughlin
(Tara Mitchell), Theresa Saldana (Rhonda), Trinidad
Silva (Tito), Suzanne Snyder (Lisa), Morgan Lofting
(Mom), Gwil Richards (Dad), Chris Hebert (Brother)

Dangerous Liaisons (1988)
UK/USA 120 minutes
Directed by Stephen Frears
Screenplay by Christopher Hampton, based on his
play from the book *Les Liaisons Dangereuses* by
Choderlos De Laclos
Production Company: Lorimar Film Entertainment/NFH
Productions/Warner Brothers
Cast: Glenn Close (Marquise De Merteuil), John
Malkovich (Vicomte De Valmont), Uma Thurman
(Cecile De Volanges), Michelle Pfeiffer (Madame De
Tourvel), Swoosie Kurtz (Madame de Volanges),
Keanu Reeves (Chevalier Darceny) Mildred Natwick
(Madame De Rosemonde), Peter Capaldi (Azolan), Joe
Sheridan (Georges)

Life Under Water (1988)
USA 1988 90 minutes
Directed by Jay Holman
Screenplay by Richard Greenberg, based on his own
play
Production Company: American Playhouse
Cast: Keanu Reeves, Sarah Jessica Parker, Haviland
Morris, Joanna Gleason, Stephen McHattie

Parenthood (1988)
USA 1989 124 minutes
Directed by Ron Howard
Screenplay by Lowell Ganz, Ron Howard and Babaloo
Mandel
Production Company: Universal Pictures
Cast: Steve Martin (Gil), Mary Steenburgen (Karen),
Dianne Wiest (Helen), Jason Robards (Frank), Rick
Moranis (Nathan), Tom Hulce (Larry), Martha Plimpton
(Julie), Keanu Reeves (Tod), Harley Jane Kozak (Susan)

I Love You to Death (1989)
USA 1989 96 minutes
Directed by Lawrence Kasdan
Screenplay by John Kostmayer
Production Company: Chestnut Hill/TriStar
Cast: Kevin Kline (Joey), Tracey Ullman (Rosalie), Joan
Plowright (Nadja), River Phoenix (Devo Nod), William
Hurt (Harlan), Keanu Reeves (Marlon)

Aunt Julia and the Scriptwriter (1989)
(AKA Tune in Tomorrow)
USA 1989 102 minutes
Directed by Jon Amiel
Screenplay by William Boyd, based on the novel by
Mario Vargas Llosa
Production Company: Cinecom
International/Odyssey/Polar Entertainment Corporation
Cast: Barbara Hershey (Aunt Julia), Keanu Reeves
(Martin Loader), Peter Falk (Pedro Carmichael), Bill
McCutcheon (Puddler), Patricia Clarkson (Aunt Olga),
Richard Portnow (Uncle Luke)

Point Break (1990)
USA 1990 122 minutes
Directed by Kathryn Bigelow
Screenplay by W. Peter Iliff and Rick King
Production Company: Largo Entertainment
Cast: Patrick Swayze (Bodhi), Keanu Reeves (Johnny
Utah), Gary Busey (Pappas), Lori Petty (Tyler), John C.
McGinley (Ben Harp)

My Own Private Idaho (1990)
USA 1990 102 minutes2
Directed by Gus Van Sant
Screenplay by Gus Van Sant, inspired by William
Shakespeare's *Henry IV*
Production Company: New Line Cinema
Cast: River Phoenix (Mike Waters), Keanu Reeves
(Scott Favor), James Russo (Richard Waters), William
Richert (Bob Pigeon), Rodney Harvey (Gary), Chiara
Caselli (Carmella), Michael Parker (Digger), Jessie
Thomas (Denise), Flea (Budd), Grace Zabriskie
(Alena), Udo Kier (Hans)

Bill and Ted's Bogus Journey (1991)
USA 1991 98 minutes
Directed by Peter Hewitt
Screenplay by Chris Matheson and Ed Solomon
Production Company: Columbia Pictures/Interscope
Communications
Cast: Keanu Reeves (Ted 'Theodore' Logan), Alex
Winter (Bill S. Preston/Granny), William Sadler (Grim
Reaper), Joss Ackland (De Nomolos)

Bram Stoker's Dracula (1991)
USA 1991 122 minutes
Directed by Francis Ford Coppola
Written by James V. Hart, from the novel by Bram
Stoker
Production Company: Columbia Pictures/American
Zoetrope/Osiris Films
Cast: Gary Oldman (Dracula), Winona Ryder (Mina
Murray/Elisabeta), Anthony Hopkins (Professor
Abraham Van Helsing/Chesare), Keanu Reeves
(Jonathan Harker), Richard E. Grant (Doctor Jack
Seward), Cary Elwes (Lord Arthur Holmwood)

Freaked (1992)
(AKA Hideous Mutant Freakz)
USA 1992 86 minutes
Directed by Alex Winter and Tom Stern
Written by Tim Burns, Alex Winter and Tom Stern
Production Company: Pandora/20th Century Fox
Cast: Alex Winter (Ricky Coogin), Brooke Shields
(Skye Daley), William Sadler (Dick Brian), Morgan
Fairchild (Stewardess), Randy Quaid (Elijah C. Skuggs),
Mr. T (The Bearded Lady), Keanu Reeves (Ortiz the
Dog Boy, uncredited)

Much Ado About Nothing (1992)
USA 1992 111 minutes

Directed by Kenneth Branagh
Written by Kenneth Branagh, based on the play by
William Shakespeare
Production Company: British Broadcasting Corporation
(BBC)/Renaissance Films/Samuel Goldwyn Company
Cast: Richard Briers (Seigneur Leonato, Governor of
Messina), Kate Beckinsale (Hero), Imelda Staunton
(Margaret), Jimmy Yuill (Friar Francis), Brian Blessed
(Seigneur Antonio), Phyllida Law (Ursula), Emma Thompson
(Beatrice), Alex Lowe (Messenger), Denzel Washington (Don
Pedro of Aragon), Keanu Reeves (Don John)

Even Cowgirls Get the Blues (1992)
USA 1992 96 minutes
Directed by Gus Van Sant
Screenplay by Gus Van Sant, based on the novel by
Tom Robbins
Production Company: Fourth Vision/New Line Cinema
Cast: Uma Thurman (Sissy Hankshaw), John Hurt (The
Countess), Rainbow Phoenix (Bonanza Jellybean), Pat
Morita (The Chink), Keanu Reeves (Julian), Lorraine
Bracco (Delores Del Ruby), Angie Dickinson (Miss
Adrian), Sean Young (Marie Barth), Crispin Glover
(Howard Barth), Ed Begley Jr. (Rupert), Carol Kane (Carla)

Little Buddha (1992)
USA 1992 140 minutes
Directed by Bernardo Bertolucci
Screenplay by Bernardo Bertolucci, Mark Peploe, Rudy
Wurlitzer
Production Company: CiBy 2000
Cast: Keanu Reeves (Siddhartha), Ying Ruocheng (Lama
Norbu), Chris Isaak (Dean Conrad), Bridget Fonda (Lisa
Conrad), Alex Wiesendanger (Jesse Conrad)

Speed (1993)
USA 1993 115 minutes (special edition: 143 minutes)
Directed by Jan De Bont
Screenplay by Graham Yost (Joss Whedon, uncredited)
Production Company: 20th Century Fox
Cast: Keanu Reeves (Jack Traven), Dennis Hopper
(Howard Payne), Sandra Bullock (Annie), Joe Morton
(Capt. Herb McMahon), Jeff Daniels (Harry Temple),
Alan Ruck (Stephens), Glen Plummer (Jaguar Owner),
Richard Lineback (Norwood)

Johnny Mnemonic (1994)
USA 1994 103 minutes
Directed by Robert Longo
Screenplay by William Gibson
Production Company: Cinevision/Alliance
Communications/TriStar
Cast: Keanu Reeves (Johnny Mnemonic), Dina Meyer
(Jane), Ice-T (J-Bone), 'Beat' Takeshi Kitano
(Takahashi), Denis Akiyama (Shinji), Dolph Lundgren
(Street Preacher), Henry Rollins (Spider), Barbara
Sukowa (Anna Kalmann), Udo Kier (Ralphy), Tracy
Tweed (Pretty)

A Walk in the Clouds (1994)
USA 1994 102 minutes
Directed by Alfonso Arau
Screenplay by Robert Mark Kamen, Mark Miller,
Harvey Weitzman, based on the film *Quattro passi fra
le nuvole*, screenplay by Piero Tellini, Cesare Zavattini,
Vittorio de Benedetti
Production Company: 20th Century Fox/Zucker
Brothers Production
Cast: Keanu Reeves (Paul Sutton), Aitana Sanchez-
Gijon (Victoria Aragon), Anthony Quinn (Don Pedro
Aragon), Giancarlo Giannini (Alberto Aragon),
Angelica Aragon (Marie Jose Aragon)

Feeling Minnesota (1995)
USA 1995 90 minutes
Directed by Steven Baigelman
Screenplay by Steven Baigelman
Production Company: Fine Line/Jersey Films
Cast: Keanu Reeves (Jjaks Clayton), Vincent D'Onofrio
(Sam Clayton), Cameron Diaz (Freddie), Dan Aykroyd
(Ben Costikyan), Courtney Love (Waitress), Tuesday
Weld (Norma Clayton)

Chain Reaction (1996)
USA 1996 106 minutes
Directed by Andrew Davis
Screenplay by Michael Bortman, Josh Friedman, J.F.
Lawton, Arne Schmidt, Rick Seaman
Production Company: 20th Century Fox/Chicago

Pacific Entertainment
Cast: Keanu Reeves (Eddie Kasalivich), Rachel Weisz
(Dr Lily Sinclair), Morgan Freeman (Paul Shannon), Fred
Ward (Ford), Kevin Dunn (FBI Agent Doyle), Brian Cox
(Lyman Earl Collier), Joanna Cassidy (Maggie)

The Last Time I Committed Suicide (1996)
USA 1996 92 minutes
Directed by Stephen Kay
Screenplay by Stephen Kay, based on a letter by Neal
Cassady
Production Company: Bates Entertainment/Kushner-
Locke Co/Tapestry Films/K1/7 Venture
Cast: Thomas Jane (Neal Cassady), Keanu Reeves
(Harry), Tom Bower (Captain), Adrien Brody (Ben),
Joe Doe (Lew), Claire Forlani (Joan), Marg
Helgenberger (Lizzy), Gretchen Mol (Cherry Mary)

Devil's Advocate (1997)
USA 1997, 110 minutes
Directed by Taylor Hackford
Screenplay by Lawrence D. Cohen, Tony Gilroy,
Robert Mark Kamen, and Jonathan Lemkin, based on
the novel by Andrew Neiderman
Production Company: Warner Bros./New Regency/
3 Arts
Cast: Al Pacino (John Milton), Keanu Reeves (Kevin
Lomax), Charlize Theron (Mary Ann Lomax), Delroy
Lindo, Craig T. Nelson, Jeffrey Jones, Judith Ivey,
Ruben Santiago-Hudson, Neal Jones, Connie Nielson